C000144126

Home Games for the People

$\frac{1\,8\,3}{}$

MOMBERGER E.BALDWINE

THE FEATHER.

HOME GAMES

FOR

THE PEOPLE:

A COLLECTION OF FAMILY AMUSEMENTS FOR THE FIRE-
SIDE, PARLOUR, OR PIC-NIC PARTIES;

CONSISTING OF

Games of Action ; Games simply taxing the Attention ; Catch Games, depending
on the assistance of an Accomplice ; Games requiring the Exercise
of Fancy, Memory, Intelligence, and Imagination.

For the Use of the Old and Young.

LIBRARY OF CONGRESS 1871 CITY OF WASHINGTON

NEW YORK:

PHILIP J. COZANS,

NO. 107 NASSAU STREET,
Corner of Ann.

GV1471
.H7

ENTERED according to Act of Congress in the year 1855,
BY PHILIP J. COZANS,
In the Clerk's Office of the District Court of the United States,
for the Southern District of New York.

VINCENT L. DILL, Stereotyper,
198 Fulton Street, New York.

CONTENTS.

―――――

I. Games of Action.

iv   CONTENTS.

II. Games simply Taxing the Attention.

III. Games of Memory.

CONTENTS.

CONTENTS.

CONTENTS.

Forfeits, &c.

CONTENTS.

GAMES OF ACTION.

HOT COCKLES.

FORTUNATELY the principles of this game of our ancestors are more easily explained than its title, whose origin is lost in the midst of antiquity.

A player kneels down before a lady, concealing his face in her lap, as for the crying of forfeits. He then places one hand, with the palm uppermost, on his back. The rest of the company advance in turns, each administering to the open hand a slap. The task of the kneeler is to discover (without looking up) who it is has given the slap. Should he succeed, the detected player takes his place; if not, he continues to occupy it himself, till such time as he shall make a more fortunate guess.

The impatience of the victim, who, having received several slaps without divining the operator, hears ironical suggestions offered to him, such as, "the loan of a pair of spectacles," "a bedroom candle, as he really ought not to go to sleep *there*," a promise to "hit harder next time, that he may recognise the hand," &c., is very delightful indeed—*to the spectators.*

THE BUNDLES.

THIS is the only variety of the class of games known as "Touch," or "Tag," worthy of distinction.

The players, who must be of an even number, are formed into a double ring, their faces to the centre—a lady being placed in front of each gentleman—each pair forming what is termed a *bundle*. The *bundles* being arranged, two of the players are chosen—one to run after and touch the other. The pursued has the right of crossing the ring in any direction (for which purpose the *bundles* must be sufficiently far apart from each other to afford an easy passage), and when tired and not wishing to be touched (and consequently become *pursuer* in his turn), may rest himself by standing in front of one of the *bundles*. The *bundle* is then composed of three persons— which is not allowable. The outside one of the three must therefore run away to avoid being touched. If touched, he takes the place of his pursuer, who is chased in his turn ; or if he likes it better, places himself in front of one of the *bundles*, thereby compelling another player to run away,—as the first. The fugitive, can however, resign his post at any moment, by placing himself in front of the *bundle*. The more frequently this is done, the greater the perplexity of the pursuer ;—and in consequence, the animation of the game.

As an in-door amusement, this game is out of the question, from the space required for its exercise.

THE FEATHER.

ONE of the players takes a bed-feather, a bit of cotton-down, or any light substance coming under the comprehensive denomination of " fluff," which he tosses up in the centre of the assembled circle (who should be seated as closely together as convenience will admit of). He then blows upon it to keep it floating in the air. The individual to whom it comes nearest does the same in order to prevent its falling on his knees, or indeed any part of his person—an accident which would subject him to the payment of a forfeit.

One of the chief advantages of this simple but highly amusing game is, that steady serious people may be in-

duced to engage in it. The gravity of their faces, blow-
ing and puffing away at the contemptible feather, as if.
all their hopes were centred in evading its responsibility,
is truly edifying. Sometimes it happens (it being impossible to blow and laugh at the same time) that the
" fluff," drops into the player's mouth at the very moment when he is concentrating all his energies in the
effort to get rid of it. This is the signal for shouts of
laughter, and for a forfeit demanded in just expiation of
the player's greediness. We recollect seeing an eminent
college dignitary in such a predicament—a spectacle not
without its instructive tendencies.

JACK'S ALIVE.

THE players pass from one to another a lighted match
or twist of paper, of which the flame has been blown out,
saying (as they present it), " *Jack's alive !* "
The player in whose hands the last spark dies out pays
a forfeit; for which reason, when " Jack " appears in a
tolerably lively condition you do not hurry yourself to
give it up. When, on the contrary, the sparks seem inclined to die out you lose no time in handing it to your

neighbour, who is bound to receive it directly you have pronounced the requisite words.

This very simple game affords considerable amusement without in the least degree taxing the intellectual resources of the players.

THE WOLF AND THE LAMBS.

IN this game, all the ladies of a company may participate, but only one gentleman at a time—who should be a man of dauntless courage and great powers of endurance.

This latter personage is called the *Wolf*. The principal lady takes the part of the *Shepherdess*. The others stand behind her in a single file, and constitute the *Flock*.

The aim of the Wolf is to catch the innocent lamb who may happen to be at the extremity of the flock. He, however, manifests his hostile intentions by the following terrible announcement!

"I am the Wolf! the Wolf! Come to eat you all up."

The Shepherdess replies, "I am the Shepherdess, and will protect my lambs."

The Wolf retorts, "I'll have the little white one with the golden hoofs."

This dialogue concluded, the Wolf attempts to make

an irruption in the line of the flock. But the Shepherdess extending her arms, bars his passage. If he succeeds
in breaking through, the lamb placed at the end aban-
dons her post before he can catch her, and places herself
in front of the Shepherdess, where she incurs no risk;
and so on with the others in succession, till the Shepherdess finds herself the last of the row.

The game then finishes. The unlucky wolf pays as
many forfeits as he has allowed lambs to escape him.

If, on the contrary, he has contrived to seize one of
them, he does not eat her, but has the privilege of kissing her,* and compels her to pay a forfeit.

This game, in company with cricket, skittles, steeple-
chasing and others, is more adapted to the open air than
the precincts of an expensively furnished drawing-room.

---

* We believe that in what a popular writer has called "the present
strict state of society and mammas," great objections exist to the introduction of " kissing" in games. To silence them all—and keep up that
tremendously exalted tone for which our work intends to be celebrated—
we hereby announce that all games requiring the introduction of the objectionable ceremony, are intended by us to be played exclusively in family parties, consisting of brothers, sisters, maiden aunts, grandmothers,
and uncles. Cousins may be admitted under certain restrictions—but
the privilege can extend no farther. We hope none of our readers will
think of breaking through this regulation. If they do, all we can say is,
we can't help it. We have done our best.

THE GAME OF THE KEY.

THIS game may be played by any number of persons, who should all, except one, seat themselves on chairs placed in a circle, and he should stand in the centre of the ring. Each sitter must next take hold, with his left hand, of the right wrist of the person sitting on his left, being careful not to obstruct the grasp by holding the hands. When all have, in this manner, joined hands, they should begin moving them from left to right, making a circular motion, and touching each other's hands, as if for the purpose of taking something from them. The player in the centre then presents a *key* to one of the sitters, and turns his back, so as to allow it to be privately passed to another, who hands it to a third ; and thus *the key* is quickly handed round the ring from one player to the other; which task is easily accomplished, on account of the continued motion of the hands of all the players. Mean- while, the player in the centre, after the key has reached the third or fourth player, should watch its progress narrowly, and endeavour to seize it in its passage. If he succeed, the person in whose hand it is found, after pay- ing a forfeit, must take his place in the centre, and give and hunt the key in his turn ; should the seeker fail in discovering the key in his first attempt, he must continue his search until he succeeds. When a player has paid three forfeits, he is out.

SNAP DRAGON

Is another Chrismas pastime. A dish of raisins being prepared, some heated brandy or spirits of wine is poured over the fruit, and then set on fire, the other lights in the room being extinguished. The young folks then stand round the dish to pluck out the lighted raisins, and eat them as hastily as they can, but rarely without warming their hands and mouths. The blue flames of the burning spirit, and the singular and spectral appearance which they give to the faces of the busy crowd, are a source of considerable merriment.

PUSS, PUSS IN THE CORNER.

THIS is a very simple game, but a very lively and amusing one. In each corner of the room, or by four trees which form nearly a square, a little girl is stationed ; another one stands in the centre, who is called Puss. At the words, "Puss, puss in the corner!" they all start and run to change corners; and at the same time the one in the middle runs to take possession of the corner before the others can reach it. If she succeed in getting to the corner first, the one who is left out is obliged to become the puss. If A and B undertake to exchange corners, and A gets into B's corner, but puss gets into A's, then B must stand in the centre. In order to avoid confusion and knocking each other down, it is well to agree in what direction you will run, before the racing begins. If a little girl remains puss after three or four times going round the room, they sometimes agree that she shall pay a forfeit.

THE SHEPHERD AND THE WOLF.

THE company stand in a file, holding by each other's dresses, and are called lambs; one little girl at the head is called the shepherdess; one stands outside, and is called the wolf. As the latter walks round, the shepherdess calls out, "Who is round my house this dark night?" The one on the outside answers, "A wolf! a wolf!" The shepherdess says, "Let my lambs alone." The wolf answers, "There is one little one I will take," at the same time trying to take away the little girl at the bottom of the file. The shepherdess springs forward to stop her: the lambs all follow the motion of the shepherdess; the wolf tries to profit by the general confusion—she pretends to jump to the left, and then suddenly darts to the right. If any one gets caught, she must pay a forfeit. Sometimes one gets caught, and slips away; in that case she must run and place herself before the shepherdess for safety. When this happens, she must take upon herself the troublesome employment of the shepherdess; the wolf, likewise, loses her place, and pays a forfeit. The last lamb in the file takes the place of the wolf.

THE HUNTSMAN.

THIS game is one of the liveliest winter's evening pastimes that can be imagined: it may be played by any number of persons above four. One of the players is styled the "huntsman," and the others must be called after the different parts of the dress or accoutrements of a sportsman; thus, one is the coat, another the hat, whilst the shot, shot-belt, powder, powder-flask, dog, and gun, and every other appurtenance belonging to a huntsman, has its representative. As many chairs as there are players, excluding the "huntsman," should next be ranged in two rows, back to back, and all the players must then seat themselves.; and, being thus prepared, the "huntsman" walks round the sitters, and calls out the assumed name of one of them : for instance, "Gun !" when that player immediately gets up, and takes hold of the coat-skirts of the "huntsman," who continues his walk, and calls out all the others, one by one ; each must take hold of the skirts of the player before him, and when they are all summoned, the huntsman sets off running round the chairs as fast as he can, the other players holding on and running after him. When he has run round two or three times, he shouts out "Bang !" and immediately sits down on one of the chairs, leaving his followers to scramble to the other seats as they best can. Of course, one must be left standing, there being one chair less than the number of players, and the player so left must pay a forfeit. The game is continued until all have paid three forfeits, when they are cried, and the punishments or penances declared. The huntsman is not changed throughout the game, unless he gets tired of his post.

THE CAT AND THE MOUSE.

ALL the company stand hand in hand, in a circle; one is placed inside, called the mouse; another outside, called the cat. They begin by turning round rapidly, raising their arms; the cat springs in at one side, and the mouse jumps out at the other; they then suddenly lower their arms, so that the cat cannot escape. The cat goes round mi-au-ing, trying to get out : and as the circle are obliged to keep dancing round all the time, she will find a weak place to break through, if she is a sharp-sighted cat. As soon as she gets out, she chases the mouse, who tries to save herself by getting within the circle again. For this purpose, they raise their arms; if she gets in without being followed by the cat, the cat must pay a forfeit, and try again; but if the mouse is caught, she must pay a forfeit. They then name who shall succeed them; they fall into the circle, and the game goes on.

CONVERSATION CARDS.

CONVERSATION Cards, are well known, and may be had at any stationer's. These specimens, however, are generally characterized by the scarcely differing (in sense any more than sound) objectionable qualities of sameness and tameness. Moreover, we do not consider the amusement worth the preparation of a premeditated purchase. Such things should be got up on the spur of the moment, *and by ourselves*, or not at all.

The following are the principles on which Conversation Cards are composed :—

On a given number of blank cards you write the same number of questions. An equal number of answers are prepared, so contrived that each answer will apply to any one of the questions, in whatever order they may be asked. The questions are given to a gentleman ; the answers to a lady, or *vice versâ*. Both shuffle their cards, and the holder of the questions reads them out in succession as they come to his hand,—the other reading an answer to each in like manner. This produces replies often of a sufficiently *piquante* nature.

Examples.

QUESTION. Are you of an affectionate disposition ?
ANSWER. Before dinner.
Q. Can you weep at a tale of suffering
A. With new boots on.
Q. Do you understand the language of flowers ?
A. Three times a week, if my mother has no objection.

QUESTION. Can you keep a secret?

ANSWER. You'd laugh if I told you.

Q. Do you love the being who adores you?

A. Get out.

Q. Can your temper be trusted?

A. Under the rose.

Q. Do you sympathize with the Hungarian refugees?

A. On the top of the monument.

Q. Do you think you could love me to distraction?

A. Don't if you please.

Q. Do you often change your mind?

A. Don't you wish you may get it.

Q. May I hope?

A. Nonsense. &c. &c.

BLIND MAN'S BUFF—ITS VARIOUS MODIFICATIONS AND DERIVATIONS.

THE original (and perhaps the most amusing) form of Blind Man's Buff, is too well known to need description. Variety, however, is charming. The following are a few varieties, all more or less so in their way.

BLIND MAN IN THE CHAIR.

The players are seated on chairs sufficiently near to

each other, forming a circle. The person fixed upon by vote or otherwise, to officiate as a blind man, is deprived of sight in the usual manner :—if a gentleman, the handkerchief is applied to his eyes by a lady, and *vice versâ*.

The blind man having answered satisfactorily all questions respecting the number of fingers held up, or gone through any other ordeal that may be considered necessary, to prove that he can see nothing, is turned loose in the centre of the circle.

The players then change places rapidly so as to put his memory at fault, as to where each is seated. He then approaches the players, and without touching with his hand, (that being strictly prohibited), seats himself gently on the extremity of the knees of the first person he meets with ; and, without feeling the garments, or using any means but his own powers of guessing, assisted by the laughs around him, the rustling of stuffs, &c., must discover and pronounce the name of the person on whose knees he has seated himself.

If he guesses correctly, the discovered player takes his place, receives the handkerchief, and proceeds in the same manner. If not the players clap their hands to apprize him of his mistake, which having recognised, he proceeds to the knees of another.

It is customary for the players, in order to throw as many difficulties as possible in the way of the blind man,

to resort to little stratagems; some cover their knees
with the skirts of their neighbours' dresses; others put
sofa cushions, &c., on their laps. Ladies in silk, put
woollen shawls, &c., over their dresses. In short, every
body tries to conceal his identity as much as possible.

In case of a laudable tendency, to "pity the Poor
Blind" from the overwhelming difficulties of his position,
or a wish to give all the players a turn, it is allowable
under certain circumstances, to give him a hint as to the
name he ought to pronounce, and so put an end to his
darkened career.

SHADOW BUFF.

This version is an illustration of the proverb, "None
are so blind as those who will not see." Here the eyes
of the practitioner are not bandaged. It is, however,
the object of his comrades to make them of as little use
to him as if they were.

A sheet or white table-cloth is hung upon a screen,
after the manner of preparations for a magic lantern.
The blind man (as we may call him for the sake of distinction) is seated on a stool, low enough to prevent his
shadow being thrown on the sheet before him. At some
distance behind him a lighted candle is placed, all the
other lights in the room being extinguished.

These preparations being concluded, all the members

of the company form themselves into a sort of procession, and pass one after the other between the blind man (who is not allowed to turn his head round as much as an inch) and the table whereon the candle is placed. This produces the effect intended. The light of the candle, intercepted by the forms passing before it, throws on to the sheet a profile shadow of each.

As these shadows pass before him in succession, the blind man is obliged to declare aloud the name of the person to whom he imagines the shadow to belong ; the mistakes he falls into causing considerable amusement among the players.

It is scarcely necessary to say, that each, in passing before the light, takes all possible pains to disguise his appearance, his height and his walk, so as to prevent recognition.

It is not customary to exact forfeits at this game ; they might, however, be enforced from the players whose portraits may be recognised. By this means a new interest may be added to the game

THE BLIND MAN'S WAND.

The blind man's wand may be easily played in a drawing-room.

The blind man (in this instance really blinded, as for the primitive form of the game) is placed in the middle of the room, a light cane or other similar implement, having been given to him. The players form a circle and dance round him, holding each other's hands, enlivening the proceeding by the chorus of any popular melody that may be approved of. The chorus finished, all stand still. The blind man holds out his wand at hazard, the person to whom it is pointed being obliged to take hold of it by the end presented to him. The blind man then utters three cries, which the holder of the wand is obliged to imitate in the same tone of voice. If the latter does not know how to disguise his voice, he is detected, and takes the place of the blind man. If not, the game is resumed with a new round, and so on *ad libitum.*

HUNT THE SLIPPER.

THIS well-known game, or rather "romp," is usually played in a circle seated on the ground, in which case, it is more adapted to the lawn or park, than the drawing-room.

It may, however, be played in-doors, the company being seated on chairs. It is advisable that there should be an uneven number of players. The one fixed on to commence the game remains standing. The rest form a

circle (a lady and a gentleman being placed alternately)
in the centre of which all their toes meet. The legs however, should not be stretched out quite straight, but bent
a little at the knee so as to form a sort of circular gallery
for the passage of the slipper. When all have taken
their seats, the player standing up throws the slipper
into the centre of the circle. A hand seizes it and passes
it round under the gallery. It is the *hunter's* duty to
keep his eyes about him, to watch where it goes to, for
it often travels a long way before he can catch a trace of
it. From time to time, when he is observed to be com-
pletely *off the scent*, one of the players draws the slipper
from its hiding place, and raps the heel of it three times
against the floor ; then while the hunter is running to
catch it, passes it quickly round again to his neighbours,
who, whenever they see a fitting opportunity, repeat the
some ceremony. Frequently there is no time to pass it
round the circle ; in which case, the holder throws it into
the centre,—when it is caught by the most alert, and
put in circulation as before.

If the hunter, tired of ducking and leaping around the
circle, renounces so fatiguing a chase of his own free
will, he pays a forfeit, and receives from each player a rap
from the heel of the slipper on the head, or (if considered
invulnerable in that quarter, from the known thickness
of the material) on the knuckles. If on the contrary, he

succeeds in catching the slipper, he takes the place of the player who has suffered him to do so; and who in turn has to give chase,—of course after having paid a forfeit.

This game being, as we have already said, nothing more or less than a downright romp, it should only be played in family parties, or among the most intimate friends where the bounds of gentleness and propriety are sure not to be exceeded.

II. GAMES SIMPLY TAXING THE ATTENTION.

THE BIRDCATCHER.

THIS game is strongly recommended to families, where the gentleman next door is not an invalid, and the baby sleeps at the top of the house.

A Birdcatcher is appointed. He forms the centre of an admiring circle, composed of the entire strength of the company, seated on chairs. Each of the players (exclusive of the Birdcatcher) takes the name of a bird—as *Goose, Tom-tit, Eagle, Parrot, Wren, Duck, Canary,* &c. The selection of species is a perfectly optional matter, with one exception—there must be an *Owl* in the collection. The imperative necessity of this will be seen hereafter.

The Birdcatcher tells a story—introducing the names of the various birds as often as possible. Every bird, when his name is mentioned, must immediately utter the crow, screech, chirrup, or splutter, peculiar to his species,

with the accuracy usual in such representations; the slightest delay or mistake to be punished by a forfeit.

So long as the OWL is not mentioned, all the players sit
with their hands before them, resting on their knees. At
the first mention of his name, all hands (literally) must
get up and hide behind their owner's backs to avoid
being caught by the Birdcatcher, who is on the watch.
If, after having named the owl, he succeed in seizing a
hand not yet raised from the owner's knee, the individual so entrapped pays a forfeit, and becomes Birdcatcher
in his turn (the late official taking his name and position
in the aviary). If, on the contrary, the players are too
quick for him, and he cannot make a single capture, *he*
pays a forfeit and continues his narrative. The birds, at
the first name pronounced, replace their hands on their
knees—not till then.*

How the owl came to occupy this important position,
we are at a loss to conceive. These, however are grave
matters which we have no right to enquire into. We
should remark, by the way, that his distinguished attri-
butes do not exempt him from the common lot. When
named by the Birdcatcher, he must give his cry as well
as the rest, enjoying no more immunity from the usual
penalties than the merest tom-tit—which is consoling.

* A sharp Birdcatcher will probably name the OWL twice running.
No notice should be taken of the second mention.

When the Birdcatcher names "*all the birds in the air*," all utter their respective cries at once. Any bird neglecting to do so, or forgetting his identity and uttering the cry of another bird, pays a forfeit, as must the Birdcatcher himself in case of his inadvertently naming a bird not in the collection.

An arrangement may be come to that when he has paid a certain number he may be at liberty to resign his post—his successor to be appointed by lots, unless a Curtius-like individual can be found to throw himself into the *vacuum* for the public good.

As we have already stated, the selection of birds (with the exception of the OWL) is purely an optional matter. The exact sounds to be uttered will depend on the amount of ornithological knowledge and imitative powers possessed by the player. To prevent mistakes, however, it will be as well, on commencing the game, for each to give a specimen of the sort of thing he considers a fair illustration of his peculiar department of natural history. On the principal of the distinguished artist who wrote under his picture, "This is a house—this is a tree, &c.," the advantages of such an arrangement are too obvious to need pointing out.

The following is a list of the most available birds, with their various modes of expressing themselves—compiled from the most unquestionable authorities ;

The Cock.—" Cock-a-doodle-doo !"
The Canary. " Pretty Dick."
The Turkey. " Gobble-obble-obble."
The Magpie. " Jack wants his dinner."
The Sparrow. " Chip ! Chip !"
The Duck. " Quack ! quack ! quack !"
The Curlew. " Pe-wit ! pe-wit !"
The Parrot. " Pretty Poll."
The Crow. " Caw ! caw ! caw !"
The Owl. " To-whit ! to-whit ! to-whoo !"
The Goose. " Hiss-s-s-s !"
The Raven. " Cro-a-ak !"

These may be varied according to the humour of the
performers. The Parrot and Magpie may express themselves in any facetious terms, founded on observation or
satire. The Raven may be made to say " Never more !"
after the celebrated bird in Mr. Poe's poem. These cor-
rections must, however, be properly understood before
the commencement of the game and rigidly adhered to.

Considerable amusement may be excited by giving the
different players the names of appropriate birds. For
instance, the Duck should be either a very nice young
lady—or a gentleman in the medical profession. A gentleman remarkable for his learning, will represent the
Owl adequately ; a young lady with a nice voice the
Nightingale (whose song may be represented by a few

bars from one of Jenny Lind's popular melodies) ; a talk-ative individual the Magpie ; and so on.

Several foreign birds may be happily introduced. We have recently heard of an Australian specimen called the *Laughing Jackass,* on account of his uttering a sound something between a laugh and a bray. This should ob-viously fall to the lot of the funny man of the party. There is another known as the *More Pork* bird, from his distinct pronunciation of those two words. Any young gentleman, having expressed an anxiety as to how long it will be before supper is ready, might be selected for this. Unmistakable Geese are to be found in most parties.

All preliminaries agreed on, the Birdcatcher commen-ces his narrative something in the following manner :—

"I went out the other morning with my gun and nets to catch a few birds. I didn't intend poaching, much less robbing a farm-yard, but just on the top of a railing I saw a fine young Cock. ('*Cock-a-doodle-doo!*') There was nobody looking and I couldn't resist it when all of a sudden up came an enormous TURKEY, ('*Gobble-obble-obble!*') 'Oh! ho!' said I, 'a TURKEY! ('*Gobble-obble-obble!*') Well, a TURKEY ('*Gobble-obble-obble!*')* is worth

---

* These repetitions are quite right and proper, being generally un-foreseen—and seldom fail in bringing in forfeits—the sole aim and end of the right-minded Birdcatcher.

rather more than a wretched SPARROW, (' *Chip ! Chip !*')
and there's more to eat on it than on a CANARY. (' *Pretty
Dick !*') And as I'd made up my mind to steal a COCK,
(' *Cock-a-doodle-doo !*'), why not a GOOSE (' *Hiss-s-s !*') or a
TURKEY? (' *Gobble-obble-obble !*') I crept up to him, when all
of a sudden, a rascally MAGPIE (' *Jack wants his dinner !*')
flew out of a bush making such an abominable noise that
ALL THE BIRDS IN THE AIR† (*general cry, without moving
the hands*)—took flight at once. Off went the TURKEY
(' *Gobble-obble-obble !*') on one side, and the COCK (' *Cock-
a-doodle-doo !*') on the other, scattering a complete flock of
DUCKS. (' *Quack ! Quack !*') There wasn't a single bird
in sight, except an OWL. (' *To-whit ! to-whit ! to-whoo !*'
—*All hands up. A forfeit given either by the unlucky Birdcatcher, who has not succeeded in catching a hand, or by a
bird whose hand he has caught. In either case, he who remains or becomes Birdcatcher continues:*)—As I was saying,
the OWL (*dead silence—all hands still up*) suddenly began
making such an extraordinary noise, no doubt thinking
himself a NIGHTINGALE (*the nightingale sings a few bars
from the ' Daughter of the Regiment ;' all hands down on
the knees immediately. Forfeits from those too late, or in
too great a hurry to replace them*) that ALL THE BIRDS IN

† The Birdcatcher can generally secure a few forfeits by saying *all
the birds in the hedge—in the field, &c,;* the *air* only should be attended
to as a signal.

THE AIR (*general cry*) flocked round again to see what could be the matter. Up came the SPARROW ('*Chip! chip!*') the CROW ('*Caw! caw!*') the RAVEN ('*Croak!*' or '*Never more!*' as agreed on), the wild DUCK, ('*Quack! quack!*') even the farmer's PARROT, ('*Pretty Poll!*')—in fact, ALL THE BIRDS IN THE FIELD (*dead silence*). 'Oh! ho!' I said, 'now I shall put salt on some of your feathered inexpressibles; when, to my horror the beast of an OWL —" ('*To-whit! to-whit! to-whoo!*'—*All hands disappear as before. The Birdcatcher catches or doesn't catch, &c. &c.*)

This game, which may be prolonged, *ad infinitum*, will be found highly entertaining not only to the parties engaged in it, but (if played in a front room, and conducted with proper spirit) to the boys in the street as well,—not forgetting the policeman.

THE SPORTSMAN AND THE GAME.

THE players take names of different birds and beasts of the field, such as Hare, Rabbit, Fox, Partridge, Quail, Woodcock, Boar, Stag, Wolf, Lion, &c.

One of the party is appointed the Sportsman, and makes use of certain sporting terms—naming implements, &c. connected with the various departments of the chase —to which when pronoucced, the different heads of game reply by phrases agreed on.

Thus, when he names—

The gun,

All the players cry, " Look out!   Look out!"

The greyhound,

The Hare says, " Run!   Run!"

The terrier,

The Rabbit says, To earth! To earth!"

The snare,

The Wolf and the Fox say, "Not if I know it!"

The nets,

The Lion and all the birds exclaim, " Try it! Try it!"

A thicket,

The Boar says, " Mind my tusks!"

The stag-hound,

The Stag says, "I have good legs!"

The horn,

The stag and the Fox say, " Be alive!"

The bag,

All drop their heads on their chests, as if killed—with the exception of the Lion, the Stag, and the Boar who exclaim, " Who's afraid!"

Example.

THE SPORTSMAN.

Well, I expect a good day's sport. I've cleaued up my *gun*——

ALL.

"Look out! Look out!"

THE SPORTSMAN.

James—unkennel the *terriers.*

THE RABBIT.

To earth! To earth!"

THE SPORTSMAN.

And take the *greyhounds.*

THE HARE.

"Run! Run!"

THE SPORTSMAN.

And go round to the other side of the wood to look at the *nets.*

THE LION AND ALL THE BIRDS.

"Try it! Try-it!"

THE SPORTSMAN.

I have no doubt I shall find something in the *snare.*

The Fox and the Wolf.

"Not if I know it."

The Sportsman.

But what's that in the *thicket ?*

The Boar

" Mind my tusks."

The Sportsman.

A magnificent stag, I declare. John, take back my *gun.*

All.

" Look out ! Look out !"

The Sportsman.

Saddle the horses, and bring out the *stag-hounds.*

The Stag.

" I have good legs."

The Sportsman.

Summon all the neighbours with a tremendous blast of the *horn.*

The Stag and the Fox.

" Be alive !"

The Sportsman.

And here—I shan't want my *bag*

(*All, except the* LION, *the* STAG, *and the* BOAR, *drop their heads.*)

THE LION, THE STAG, AND THE BOAR.

"Who's afraid?"

THE SPORTSMAN.

Look sharp, John—sound the *horn.*

THE STAG AND THE FOX.

" Be alive!"

THE SPORTSMAN.

We shall never catch him. He's miles away. Let's have a look at the *snare.*

THE WOLF AND THE FOX.

"Not if I know it!"

THE SPORTSMAN.

Nothing, I declare! There's not enough left to dine a *terrier.*

THE RABBIT.

"To earth! To earth!"

THE SPORTSMAN.

I shall go home—there's no sport to be had, &c. &c. &c.

Any player neglecting to pronounce the word allotted to the animal he represents, or to perform the action agreed on, pays a forfeit.

THE PAINTER AND THE COLOURS

THIS belongs to a large family, of which *The Birdcatcher*, *My Lady's Toilet*, *The Echo*, &c., will be recognised as conspicuous members.

The leader of the game is the Painter. The rest of the players are the Colours,—each taking a name,—*blue, green, orange, &c.* Beyond his own name (to which the colour when called upon must reply, by mentioning that of one of his comrades), there are four words which must be answered in various ways.

The painter is supposed to have a commission to paint a particular subject, on which he founds a discourse. When he names the *palette*, all the players (except the painter) cry out, " *Colours ! colours !*"

If he speaks of *colours* in general, all say, " *Here we are.*"

If of his *pencil*, the answer exacted is, "*Brush ! brush !*"

Finally, when he names *turpentine*, gereral consternation is excited, and the colours with one accord exclaim, " *Help ! help !*"

We have already stated that any colour mentioned by name must immediately name another of the party. The latter replies simply, " *Here sir.*" Mistake or hesitation in giving the replies, as usual, to be punished by forfeits.

Example.

THE PAINTER. I am commissioned by my noble patron, the Marquis of Carabas, to paint a picture of the *finding of the body of Harold.* It is a very impottant matter. I have made my design, and shall commence setting my *palette.*

ALL THE COLOURS. *Colours! Colours!*

THE PAINTER. I intend astonishing the critics by the brilliancy of my *colours.*

ALL. *Here we are!*

PAINTER. I can't employ you all at a time—rather a task for a single *pencil.*

ALL. *Brush! brush!*

PAINTER. Silence! or I'll exterminate you with a dose of *turpentine.*

ALL. *Help! help!*

PAINTER. Come be quiet, or I won't employ one of you. I'll begin with the eyes of the fair Edith. Hang it, I don't know what colour they were. They ought to be *black.**

BLACK. *Green! green!*

GREEN. Here, sir.

---

* If the painter names a colour not in the collection he pays a forfeit. The same rule applies to the colours.

PAINTER. No ; she was called Edith the Fair. They must have been *blue.*

BLUE. *Orange !. orange !*

ORANGE. Here, sir.

PAINTER. As she was in trouble, her cheeks ought to be pale, almost *white.*

WHITE. *Purple and cherry colour.*

PURPLE AND CHERRY (*together.*) Here, sir.

PAINTER. All the *colours*—

ALL. Here we are !

PAINTER. —Of the rainbow shall be employed to give effect to the richness of her dress, as becoming a high-born damsel ; and thanks to the delicacy of my *pencil*—

ALL. Brush ! brush ! &c. &c.

Our authority for this game (which is of French extraction) says that " the great art on the part of the colour cited, is to fix upon another likely to make the most ridiculous contrast with the subject of the picture." We question the powers of art to produce any very striking results by those means. The humour of proposing green cheeks, scarlet eyes, &c., is by no means brilliant. The success of the game, like that of many others, will therefore depend on the introduction of another species of humour, to be supplied by the player. We allude to *good humour.*

MAGIC MUSIC.

THIS game is an improvement on the old one known as *Hot boiled beans and very good butter*.

In that obsolete entertainment, it will be remembered, a bean, or other small object was concealed, and one of the players (previously sent out of the room) summoned to look for it, by the couplet—

"Hot boiled beans and very good butter,
Won't you please to come to supper?"

his only guide to the whereabouts of the hidden treasure being as follows :—In proportion as he neared or receded from it, he was said to be *hot* or *cold*,—the other players telling him which, and in what degree. When close to it, he was *burning, in the fire*, &c. When on an entirely false scent, he was *freezing*, at the *North Pole*, and so on, till the bean was found.

All this was very obvious, and very contemptible. The steam-engine, however, had its origin in a tea-kettle. This simple invention * has laid the foundation of an entertainment worthy of the enlightened age we live in.

The game as it now stands, is as follows :—

* The writer begs to state that he means the game, not the tea-kettle.

A player is sent out of the room, as heretofore, but instead of hiding a bean for him to find, the company think of a task to be performed by him. This task may be anything ;—to untie a ribbon, to sing a song, to displace all manner of articles of furniture—the more fantastic and out of the way the better. When they have decided what it is to be, the patient is summoned in, and has to set to work to discern and perform the work allotted to him. Instead of the old *hot* and *cold* regulation, he is guided in his experiments by the sounds of a piano or other musical instrument* played softly, or the reverse, in proportion to his success, or the want of it.

Those who have never played at this game can have no idea of the interest attached to it. The tasks that may be divined and accomplished, with no other clue than the threatening or encouraging tones of the music, would appear incredible. The complete bewilderment of the *guesser*, on first entering the room, as to what he is to do ; his numerous experiments, all wide of the mark ; his first catching at a hint, and gradual following of it up, with various intervening discouragements, till he has fulfilled his mission (as a player of ordinary intelligence usually does) ; furnish entertainment of a by no means unelevated description.

* In case of there being none in the room, rapping against the tongs with a pair of snu?ers or any other metalic implement will do.

Forfeits may be exacted in case of non-success. Their assistance, however, is not required to make the game interesting.

WHAT'S THE PRICE OF BARLEY?

THE conductor of the game is called the *Master*. He gives to the different players any names he likes, consisting of simple words, such as—

1. *Jack.*
2. *How much.*
3. *What.*
4. *Too much.*
5. *Bravo.*
6. *Fifty dollars.*
7. *Fifty cents.*
8. *One dime.*
9. *Good.*
10. *Nonsense.*

The game is carried on in dialogue, commencing with the Master, in the following manner :—

MASTER. *Jack !*
PLAYER No. 1. Yes, Master.

MASTER. What's the price of barley?

No. 1. Fifty dollars.

MASTER. *Good!*

No. 9. Yes, Master.

MASTER. What's the price of barley?

No. 9. One dime.

MASTER. *One dime! Nonsense!*

Nos. 8 & 10 (*together*). Yes, Master.

MASTER. *How much?*

No. 2. Yes, Master.

MASTER. What's the price of barley?

No. 2. Fifty cents.

MASTER. *Fifty cents! Bravo! Jack!*

Nos. 7, 5, & 1 (*together*). Yes, Master.

What's the price of barley?

Nos. 7, 5, & 1 (*together*). Fifty cents—Fifty dollars—One dime (or *as they may feel inclined*).

MASTER. *Nonsense!*

No. 10. Yes, Master, &c. &c.

It will be seen by the above, that the duty of each player is to answer, " *Yes, Master*," on hearing the master pronounce his adopted name. If he neglects this, he pays a forfeit, as also on answering to his name when pronounced by anybody else.

BIRDS FLY.

A VERY simple game, in which all the players place a finger on a table, or on the knees of the conductor of the game, to be raised in the air, when the conductor says, "*Birds fly*," "*Pigeons* (or any winged object in natural history) *fly*."

If he names a non-winged animal, and any player raises his hand in distraction, the latter pays a forfeit—the same in case of his neglecting to raise it at the name of a bird or winged insect.

THE ELEMENTS.

THE players form a semicircle round the king of the game, who holds in his hand a ball of thread partially unrolled and fastened by a knot, leaving a length of thread sufficient for the ball to *reach* one of the players he may choose to throw it to, and enable him to draw it back immediately. The names of three animals—each inhabiting a different one of the three elements—EARTH, AIR, or WATER, must be first decided on ; such as *dog*, *salmon*, *pigeon*. When the king touches a player with his ball of the thread, saying EARTH, AIR, or WATER, the player must respond immediately with the name of the animal inhabiting the element cited.

For instance, if the king says WATER, the person he touches immediately replies *salmon*. Should he reply *dog* or *pigeon*, he pays a fine—neither of these animals inhabiting the water.

The king may also say FIRE. A dead silence must be observed when he does so—fire not being inhabited by any animal yet discovered. Should he say THE ELEMENTS, all the players together must pronounce the names of the three animals, in quick succession.

The game may be played without fixing on the names of any particular animals ; in which case, when the king names an element, the player he touches must respond immediately with the name of an animal known to inhabit it, and not mention the same animal twice, on pain of a forfeit.

The former, however, is the most amusing method. The frequent repetition of the three names generally leading to great confusion.

THE RULE OF CONTRARY.

THE rules of this game are not intricate. All the players, standing up, take hold of the sides of a handkerchief.

The president of the game (taking hold with the rest) makes mystic circles on the handkerchief with his forefinger, exclaiming,—

"Here we go round by the rule of contrary ;* when I say 'Hold fast,' let go ; when I say ' Let go,' hold fast."

He then says " Let go," or " Hold fast," as he may feel inclined. When he says " Let go," those who do not hold fast pay forfeits ; when he says " Hold fast," all who do not immediately let go are punished in like manner.

It may be thought by those who have never attempted the game that few victims are to be caught by so simple a contrivance. We advise all harbouring such opinions to try it at the earliest opportunity.

THE TRADES.

EACH player selects a trade, which he carries on in dumb show, as follows :—

The tailor stitches a coat.

The cobbler mends a shoe.

The laundress washes imaginary tubs full of shirts.

----

* We have played at this game in various societies. The word is always pronounced con-*trairy*. We don't know why—but it is so, and we are not radicals enough to inquire into so important a matter.

The painter paints a portrait.

The blacksmith hammers at the anvil, &c. &c.

One of the party is chosen as King of the Trades, and commences the game by exercising his own—setting an example of industry to the others, who must work away indefatigably at their various callings. When the king takes it into his head to change his trade and adopt that of one of the party, all leave off work at once, and remain inactive, except the player thus imitated, who immediately takes up the trade of the king, which he continues to exercise till such a time as it shall please his majesty to change again and take up somebody else's. The individual honoured by this second choice then takes up the king's trade and continues till a third change takes place—the other players remaining idle, till the king resumes his original occupation—the signal for all to fall to work again.

Any player making a mistake pays a forfeit.

Not a bad name for this game would be *Mind your own Business.*

MY LADY'S TOILET; OR, SPINNING THE TRENCHER.

ALL the players adopt the names of various articles connected with the mistery of a Lady's Toilet,—as *Buckle, Necklace, Gloves, Bouquet, Handkerchief,* &c. &c.

A circle is formed of chairs, one less than the number of players,—one of whom is consequently without a seat.

This excluded personage commences the game. He is provided with a wooden trencher, or similar implement,* with which he advances to the centre, exclaiming,—

"My lady is going to dress for a ball, and wants so and so (her *gloves,* her *ear-rings,* or any other of the articles agreed on)."

As he pronounces the word, he gives the trencher a vigorous twist, and leaves it spinning on the ground. The player called upon, immediately darts from his seat (which is taken by the spinner), so as to catch the trencher while spinning. Should it fall to the ground before he reaches it, he pays a forfeit.

The second player then spins the trencher, announcing that my lady is in want of another article. The person named runs to catch it,—the last spinner taking his seat as before ; and so on, *ad infinitum.*

To name an article not included in the games, costs a forfeit.

The spinner may vary the proceedings occasionally, by, instead of naming any particular article, making use of

---

* The best china plates are seldom improved by being employed for this purpose. Nor can we conscientiously recommend the punch-bowl.

the word *toilet.* This is the signal for all to change places, the speaker rushing at the nearest vacant chair. Any one found after the scuffle in the same place as before it, pays a forfeit, as must also the player who is left at last without a seat at all,—who, moreover, takes the next turn at the trencher.

He may also pronounce the word *twilight,* as by saying, " My lady is going out this evening at *twilight,* &c., &c. ;" on which no one is allowed to move, on pain of a forfeit. The similarity of the two words generally leads to some of the players, in the hurry of the moment, confusing the opposite duties attached to them.

THE BOX OF SECRETS.

THIS game, which is very popular in France, under the name of *la boîte d'amourette,* is simply a means of collecting forfeits. It is played as follows :—

The player who commences the game, presents a box to his neighbour on the right, saying, " I sell you my box of secrets ; it contains three—*whom I love, whom I will kiss, and whom I will send about his (or her) business.*

The neighbour replies,—

" Whom do you love ? whom will you kiss ? whom will

you send about her business?" (We assume the giver of the box to be a gentleman.)

The first speaker names, in answer to each question, the one of the players whom he loves, the one he intends to kiss (why these should not be one and the same it is not our business to inquire into) and the one he intends to send about her business.

The person he intends to kiss is compelled to kiss him on the spot. The one to be sent about her business pays a forfeit. No notice whatever is taken of the loved one, which we are at a loss to account for, except as a satire upon professions of affection generally. In candour, however, we are compelled to confess that we do not believe anything of the kind was ever intended—which is a pity.

THE ALPHABET;

OR, I LOVE MY LOVE WITH AN A.

FORMERLY, this game was confined to the players saying in rotation, "I love my love with an A because he is AMIABLE, ARDENT, ASPIRING, AMBITIOUS," and so on, through as many letters of the alphabet as might be approved of, each player having to invest his love with a

quality beginning with the letter in question. Forfeits
were exacted,—firstly for the repetition of any quality
mentioned by a previous player ; secondly, for faults of
spelling.

As, however (thanks to the progress of education), people are no longer in the habit of loving others because
they are Andsome, Onorable, or Helegant, the latter opportunity may be said to be almost obsolete. It has
therefore been decided to improve the former, by increas-
ing the difficulty of finding words.

The game, as it is at present played, will be understood
from the following specimens :—

"I love my love with an A, because he is AFFECTION-
ATE, because his name is AUGUSTUS. I will give him an
AMETHYST, I will feed him on APPLE-TARTS, and make him
a bouquet of ANEMONES."

"I love my love with a B, because she is BEAUTIFUL,
because the name is BEATRICE I will give her a BROOCH ;
I will feed her on BERRIES ; and make her a bouquet of
BLUE-BELLS."

This form need not be strictly adhered to, we merely
offer it as a model. The leader of the game may vary it
as he thinks fit ; but whatever form he may choose to
adopt, the others must imitate closely (allowing for the
variation of sexes). Failure in this must be punished by
a forfeit ; the old regulation as to repetition and mistakes

in spelling (accidents which will happen, even now, in the best educated families) still holding good.

The whole alphabet may be gone through in this manner, if the interest of the game last long enough. It is advisable, however, to exclude the letters K, Q, X, and Z, which offer too many difficulties.

COME OUT OF THAT.

THIS game is not complicated, being confined to the following dialogue :—

"Come out of that?"

"What for ?"

"Because you have such or such a thing, and I have not."

Care must be taken not to name anything you really possess yourself, or that has been mentioned by a previous player ; that is, unless you wish to pay a forfeit.

PINCH WITHOUT LAUGHING.

IN this game each player pinches the nose of his neighbour, who must submit to the operation without laughing.

If he as much as smiles, he pays a forfeit. Of course the most strenuous exertions are made by the operators to cause him to lose his gravity.

We have heard of some designing persons in this game, blacking the tips of their finger and thumb with burnt cork, which leaves a very agreeable impression on the pinched nose. If two or three unsuspecting individuals happen to be victimized in this way, they laugh heartily, *at each other*, neither suspecting that he is an object of equal ridicule—which is not only a fine moral lesson, but also leads to the great accumulation of forfeits.

THE COMICAL CONCERT.

THIS game, when well played, is extremely diverting. The players stand in a circle, and each one agrees to imitate some instrument of music. One pretends to play upon the violin, by holding out her right hand, and moving her left as if she were drawing a bow across it. *Those who have seen Mr. Maelzel's little fiddler, will know how to do this to perfection.* Another doubles up her two hands, and puts them to her mouth, to imitate a horn; another moves her fingers on a table, as if she were playing the piano; another takes the back of a chair, and

E. BALDWIN.

PINCH WITHOUT LAUGHING.

touches the rounds, as if they were the strings of a harp ; another makes motions as if beating a drum ; another holds a stick after the manner of a guitar, and pretends to play upon it ; another appears to be turning a hand-organ; in a word, the players, if sufficiently numerous, may imitate every instrument they ever heard of. This is but half the game. Each musician, while playing, must make a sound with her mouth in imitation of her instru-ment, thus :

Rub-a-dub goes the drum.
Twang, twang, goes the harp.
Toot, too hoo, goes the horn.
Tweedle dee, tweedle dee, goes the violin, &c.

All this makes an odd jumble of movements and sounds, which is very laughable, especially if each one plays her part with animation.

In the middle of the circle stands one called the *head of the orchestra*, whose business it is to beat time to the movements of all the rest, which she does in as ridiculous a way as possible, in order to make the others laugh. In the midst of all the noise and fun, she suddenly stops, and asks abruptly, " Why don't you play better," The one she looks at must answer *instantly*, in a manner suit-able to the nature of her instrument ; that is, the drum-mer must say one of the drumsticks is broken ; the harper, that the strings are too loose ; the person playing on the piano must say one of the dampers is broken, or one of the keys makes a discord ; the flute player, that the holes are too far apart for her fingers, &c.

If they hesitate a moment, or the answer is not such as is suitable to the instrument, or if they repeat an excuse that has been already made, they must pay a forfeit. While one is answering, the other stop playing ; and all begin again as soon as she has said her say, or paid her forfeit. Then the head of the orchestra looks at some other one, and asks why she don't play better ; and so it goes on till they are weary of the game. Sometimes they make it a rule, that any one who laughs so that she cannot play her part, must pay a forfeit ; in this case there would be plenty of forfeits.

FLY AWAY, PIGEON !

THE company are ranged in a circle, with one in the centre, who places the fore-finger of her right hand upon her knee and all the others put their fore-fingers around it. If the one in the centre raises her finger, saying, at the same instant, "Fly away, pigeon!" or "Fly away, sparrow!" the others must raise their fingers in the same manner ; but if, for the sake of mischief, "she exclaims,

" Fly away, trout !" or " Fly away, elephant !" the others
must be careful not to move their fingers, else they must
pay a forfeit. That is, the fingers must all rise, if a crea
ture is mentioned that *can* fly ; and kept quiet, if a thing
which *cannot* fly is named. As it is done with great ra-
pidity, it requires quick ears and quick thoughts. Sometimes things which fly only by accident are mentioned ;
such as a feather, a leaf, a sheet of paper, thistle-down, a
veil, &c. In this case, all the players never make up
their minds soon enough ; some fingers will rise, and
some keep still ; and often debates will arise to determine
which is right. " I am sure a leaf don't fly," says one ;
"I am sure it does fly on the wind," says another, &c.
The one in the centre decides all disputed questions.
This game brings laughing and forfeits in abundance.

JUDGE AND JURY.

A CIRCLE is formed, at the head of which are placed three
on elevated seats, called the Judge and Jury. Before the
game begins, all except these three have some name or
other assigned them. Thus one will be called necklace,
another bracelets, another sash, and so on. A tin or
wooden plate lies in the centre. When the judge says,

" My lady is going out, and wants her necklace," the one
named necklace must jump up, and spin the plate round
like a top.   But there are certain rules to be observed in
doing this, which are extremely difficult. She must not
make any motion, without first asking leave of the judge.
She must say, " May I get up ?"   " May I walk ?"   " May
I stoop ?"   " May I pick up the plate ?"   " May I spin
it ?"   " Shall I break it, or shall I place it ?"   (By breaking it, she merely means letting it fall bottom-upwards.)
If she is told to break it, and it does not happen to fall
that way she must forfeit.   After the plate stops, she cannot return without first asking, " May I walk ?"   " May
I sit down ?"   A forfeit is paid for every instance of forgetfulness in these rules.   The judge proclaims the forfeits ; and after the circle have all tried their luck, the
jury go out of the room to decide in what manner they
shall be paid.   I forgot to mention, that they do not rise
in succession : they wait for the judge to say, " My lady
wants her sash, or her bracelets," &c.

III. GAMES OF MEMORY.

THE ECHO.

THIS game consists of a story told by one of the players, interrupted by an echo from the others at the mention of certain agreed-on words. These words should be the names of different articles having reference to the subject of the story.

For instance, supposing THE ADVENTURES OF A SOLDIER to be fixed on, it would be advisable to select such terms as *soldier, regiment, cannon, furlough,* and the names of various military accoutrements—*knapsack, shell-jacket, foraga-cap, bayonet, sword, uniform, cartridge-box, musket, cross-belt, &c. &c.* Each player, (with the exception of the story teller,) takes a name from the list. The story is commenced. When the narrator pronounces one of the words agreed on, the player to whom it has been allotted must echo it, in the following manner :—if pronounced only once, he must repeat it twice ; if pronounced twice,

only once. A general word, such as *accoutrements*, should
be reserved to express a number of objects together,
When this is pronounced, all the players (except *soldier,
furlough*, and all whose names do not apply to any article forming a part of a military outfit) must repeat it at
once,—subject to the rules of repetition (as to whether
once or twice) already given.

Example.

THE ADVENTURES OF CORPORAL SABERTASH.

Corporal Sabertash, a brave SOLDIER—SOLDIER (*soldier !*) in the 245th REGIMENT—(*regiment, regiment !*) having returned from the wars, was allowed a month's FUR-
LOUGH (*furlough, furlough*). His heart bounded at the
prospect of revisiting his native village, and pressing
once more to his bosom the being of whom he had never
ceased to think, even amidst the roar of the CANNON—
CANNON (*cannon*), and the clash of the SWORD—SWORD
(*sword*). He hastily equipped himself in his UNIFROM
(*uniform, uniform*), polished up his MUSKET (*musket, musket*), and strapped on his KNAPSACK—KNAPSACK (*knapsack*). "Hang your SHELL-JACKET (*shell-jacket, shell-jacket*),
and FORAGE-CAP—FORAGE-CAP (*forage-cap*)," said he, "I'll
leave them behind me and astonish them all, by appear-

ing before them in my full ACCOUTREMENTS (*accoutrements, accoutrements*)."*

He marched on for a few miles, when he made a halt. "No hurry," said he, "now. I'm not with the REGIMENT (*regiment, regiment*). I shall rest a little." So he unstrapped his KNAPSACK—KNAPSACK (*knapsack*), got rid of the most cumbrous of his ACCOUTREMENTS (*accoutrements, accoutrements*), and composed himself to a nap, under a shady oak.

He was roused by the most piercing cries. With the instinct of a SOLDIER (*soldier, soldier*), he seized his MUSKET (*musket, musket*), and marched to the spot whence the cries proceeded, with the speed of a CANNON—CANNON (*cannon*)—ball. Judge of his horror, when he beheld a young and lovely female, struggling with four masked ruffians, each with a drawn SWORD (*sword, sword*). They were endeavouring to drag her to a carriage, which stood at a little distance. Our brave SOLDIER (*soldier, soldier*) seeing their intention, attacked them with the butt end of his MUSKET—MUSKET (*musket*). Two of the ruffians fell. A desperate struggle ensued between our hero and the remaining two. Unfortunately, having left his BAYONET (*bayonet, bayonet*) under the tree, his MUSKET—MUSKET (*musket*), was of little service to him at close quarters.

* Spoken by all together with the exceptions already mentioned.

He, however, seized a SWORD (*sword, sword*) from one of
the prostrate villains, and defended himself manfully.
One fell bleeding to the earth, his scull cleft in twain.
The fourth escaped. Our hero was about to pursue him,
when the lady called on him to stay.

"For Heaven's sake, sir," she said, "incur no more
risk on my account. The recollection of his villany will
be sufficient punishment for him."

"That voice!" exclaimed our SOLDIER (*soldier, soldier*);
"can it be possible?"

The maiden started, looked in his face, and, with a loud
scream, fell fainting in his arms. It was Margaret, the
object of his early love!

"And who, dearest," inquired our SOLDIER—SOLDIER
(*soldier*), after the first rapturous greetings were over;
"were the ruffians from whom I rescued you—thanks to
this good SWORD (*sword, sword*)?"

"The three who lie there, I know not," answered Margaret. "But the one who has escaped, and was their
leader, I recognised in spite of his mask. He has long
annoyed me with his persecuting addresses, but I refused
to become his bride. Could I forget my own true SOL-
DIER—SOLDIER—(*soldier*)?"

"His name—his rank?" inquired our hero impetuously.

"His exact rank I know not, but he is, like yourself, a
SOLDIER (*soldier, soldier*)—though in a far higher station."

"His name?" repeated the corporal, clutching his MUS-KET—(*musket*) fiercely.

"Sir Reginald Mandeville!"

With a wild cry of despair our hero fell prostrate on the greensward.

It was the name of the commanding officer of his REGI-MENT (*regiment, regiment*) !

*   *   *   *   *   *

Our ill-fated hero was tried by a court-martial, for assaulting his commanding-officer, and was condemned to an ignominious death. The gallant SOLDIER (*soldier, soldier*), who had so often faced the CANNON—CANNON (*cannon*) of the enemy, fell pierced by the MUSKET (*musket, musket*) shots of his comrades. The whole REGIMENT—REGIMENT (*regiment*) attended his funeral. His ACCOU-TREMENTS (*accoutrements, accoutrements*) were buried with him.

And poor Margaret! a weapon surer than the MUSKET (*musket, musket*), keener than the SWORD—SWORD (*sword*), and more deadly than the BAYONET—BAYONET (*bayonet*), Despair! pierced her gentle bosom. She died of a broken heart, crushed by the tragic events that marked the untimely close of the corporal's FURLOUGH (*furlough, furlough*).

This touching history will serve as a model for an infinity of others. The object of the narrator should be to impart so much interest to his story as to make his hearers forget to give the echo at the proper time, or not the right uumber of times—for either of which deviations from the rule, forfeits must be rigidly exacted.

THE ANTS AND THE GRASSHOPPER.

Lots are drawn to decide which of the company shall first undertake the part of the Grasshopper. This important matter settled, the chosen individual stands up, the other players (who represents the Ants) seating themselves in a circle round him. The Grasshopper writes on a piece of paper the name of a particular grain—or other article of food suitable to his species—to which he has taken a fancy. This memorandum he conceals for the present. He then advances, with a profound salutation, to the Ants, whom he addresses something in the following manner :—

"My dear and hospitable friends, I am very hungry. Would any of you lend me a little provision of some kind to be going on with?" Then addressing some particular Ant, "You, my dear friend, I know your goodness of heart; I am sure you will help me with a trifle?"

The Ant addressed replies, " I have nothing but a grain of barley" (or any other grain according to fancy).

"Thank you, I don't care for it. And you, neighbour," addressing another Ant, " is there nothing better you can offer me ?"

" A grub."

" Thank you, I would rather not."

He begs from all the players in turn, who propose a *fly*, a *grain of wheat, oats, hayseed,* &c.—always an article which a Grasshopper might be expected to eat, and which has not been mentioned before. When he has gone all round, without the article he has written been named by any one, the Grasshopper pays a forfeit, and proceeds to his second question. If, however, one of the Ants should hit upon the identical thing, " I will take it with pleasure, neighbour," cries the Grasshopper, " and may Providence reward you." He then produces his piece of paper, proving that the article proposed was the one he had thought of; the Ant pays a forfeit, and becomes Grasshopper in his turn. Instead, however, of recommencing the game, he continues it in the following manner :—" Neighbour, (he says to an Ant) " I have eaten abundantly, thanks to the kindness of your companions. I should like a dance. What dance would you recommend ?" (The name of the dance is written down secretly as in the case of the food).

The question goes round as before—the ants proposing

various dances, such as *the polka, the fandango, the schot-
tishe, the minuet, the cachuca,* &c.* The Grasshopper treats
these suggestions (his own not being among them) with
the greatest contempt. Any player proposing a dance
previously named pays a forfeit. The Grasshopper of
course does the same, should the round terminate without
the dance of his memorandum being mentioned, and proceeds to write the third question. If, on the contrary,
an ant should hit upon the right dance, they change
places as in the first instance ; and the new Grasshopper
(having paid a forfeit) continues—

" Well, I will dance, my friends. But I see no fun in
dancing without music. What instrument would you
recommend ?"

The Ants recommend various instruments, such as the
violin, the *piano,* the *cornet,* the *harp,* &c.,†—subject to the
same conditions as the previous rounds.

The fourth Grasshopper (supposing an unlucky insect
to have hit on the identical instrument) takes up the
thread ;

* Not long ago in playing this game, we heard two little boys, of ill-
regulated minds, propose the *Kickeraboo* and the *Virginny break-down.*
They were severely reprimanded by their elder sisters.

† One of the little boys already alluded to suggested, in a low voice,
the bones. We were the only person who heard him, and we pledged
him on honour it should go no further.

The Ants reply, each in his turn—*moss, stubble, sand, clover, a rose leaf,* &c. &c.

At length the fifth and last Grasshopper puts the question.

" My good friends, I should sleep very comfortably, but for a slight misgiving. I am afraid of being pounced upon by some hungry bird. What bird do you think I have most reason to fear ?"

ANSWERS :—*The rook, the partridge, the pigeon, the lark,* &c. &c.

Should the bird whose name has been written down be mentioned, the too prophetic Ant pays a forfeit, and the game is finished. If not, the Grasshopper not only pays a forfeit, but has to put the question round a second time, then a third, and more still if necessary. Nor is that all—from the commencement of the second round he has to pay a forfeit *for every answer* till the identical bird is named. The result is generally, that the Grasshopper despairing of being able to redeem the number of forfeits, exacted from him, cries for mercy ; the pitch of mental anguish to which he is wrought keeping up the excitement of the game to the very end.

This is not so good a game as the Birdcatcher. It belongs to the same school, but is of a higher class. And we all know that in most schools there is seldom so much fun going forward in the upper classes as in the lower.

THE SCHOOLMISTRESS;

OR, MY LITTLE FINGER.

THIS is, strictly speaking, a young ladies' game, though the presence of one or two of the opposite sex would rather increase than detract from its amusement.

The players seat themselves in a semicircle, in the centre of which is a seat more elevated than the rest, for the Schoolmistress, who (having been chosen by lots or otherwise) calls upon one of the "young ladies" to stand upon a stool facing the rest of her companions, to answer certain grave accusations.

The regulations of the game will be understood from the following specimen :—

MISTRESS. You went out yesterday without my permission? Pray where did you go to?

The ACCUSED. For a walk with Miss —— (naming one of the young ladies,* who must immediately reply, "If you please, Governess," or pay a forfeit).

MISTRESS. I know where you went to. My *thumb* has told me.

* If there should be any gentlemen in the game they must on no account behave as such. All must be considered young ladies for the time being, and be addressed as " Miss." The manliest whisker cannot save an individual from his temporary effeminization.

(At the word *thumb*, the accused replies, " He knows
nothing about it ;" an answer she must repeat to all
charges, so long as the Scholmistress does not name another of her fingers.*)

MISTRESS. You went to the library, and purchased
*The Haunted Shadow, or the Calabrian Brigand of Madagas-
car.* I do not allow young ladies to read romances.

ACCUSED. *He knows nothing about it.*

MISTRESS. More than that—you were seen copying
out the love-letter of Adeliza to Ferdinando, praying him
to rescue her from the cavern of the witch Dentata.

ACCUSED. *He knows nothing about it.*

MISTRESS. You tore a leaf out of your copy-book to
write it on. My *middle finger* told me.

ACCUSED. *Don't believe him.* (The answer to be applied as long as the middle finger is in question.)

MISTRESS. You meant me, by the " witch Dentata."

ACCUSED. *Don't believe him.* Miss ——— knows to
the contrary (naming another young lady, who must immediately reply, " If you please, Governess").

MISTRESS. You changed the name of Adeliza to that
of your own, and Ferdinando to that of a young gentleman.

ACCUSED. *Don't believe him.*

* *Query.* Ought a thumb to be considered a finger ? We have nothing
but an Irish Dictionary at hand. Consult Walker.

MISTRESS.   Your cousin, an abominable young officer, with moustaches.

ACCUSED.   *Don't believe him.*

MISTRESS.   You sealed the letter with a thimble, and sent it to the post.

ACCUSED.   *Don't believe him.*   Miss ——, Miss ——, and Miss —— know better. (She names those who appear most inattentive in preference to others. These must reply, "If you please, Governess," or pay forfeits.)

MISTRESS.   To the post, I say.   My *little finger* told me all about it.

ACCUSED.   *He is a storyteller.*

ALL THE YOUNG LADIES (together).—Oh! *the naughty little finger!*

MISTRESS.   He sticks to it, however.

ACCUSED.   *He is a storyteller.*   Ask *all my schoolfellows.*

All, without speaking, hold out their hands in corroboration of the statement. (The least hesitation costs a forfeit.

MISTRESS.   He says all these young ladies are storytellers.

All get up.   Those who remain seated pay forfeits. The accused enters the ranks.   A new schoolmistress is appointed who fixes on a fresh culprit, and the game recommences.

If, however, the first schoolmistress, satisfied with the

attestation of some of the young ladies who have not moved from their seats (and have, in consequence, paid forfeits), announces that the little finger has confessed himself mistaken, she can bring forward fresh charges, which the original accused must answer, on the principles already shown.

MY GRANDMOTHER'S GARDEN.

A CIRCLE is formed, and the player best acquainted with the game addresses his nearest neighbour as follows :—

"I have been to my grandmother's garden. My grandmother's garden is a beautiful garden. In my grandmother's garden there are four corners."

Each player in succession, repeats the same phrase, not adding or omitting anything on pain of a forfeit; the next player always taking up the word before he can have time to correct an error. When the turn of the first speaker comes round again, he repeats what has been previously said ; adding to it, "In the first corner there is a rose-tree. I love you to distraction."

The others repeat not only this, but also the original phrase, paying a forfeit for each mistake.

The turn finished a second time, the leader repeats the whole ; adding, "In the second corner there is a sun-flower. I would kiss you, but I am afraid."

After the third turn, he adds, " In the third corner there is a peony. Tell me your secret."

Each player then whispers whatever he pleases in the ear of his preceding neighbour.

The fourth repetition over, the leader makes another addition.

" In the fourth corner there is a poppy. Repeat aloud what you whispered to me just now."

As the oration (which has now reached its full growth) goes round the circle, each player is compelled to divulge the secret he had previously imparted to his neighbour, in confidence—rather an embarrasing condition sometimes, for people not prepared for such an arrangement— for the company are equally amused at the secrets which are not very clear, as at those which are rather too much so.

This game will be recognised as only another version of the old *House that Jack built,*—on the model of which endless games may be formed, the leader relying upon his own invention for the sayings to be repeated.

THE HORNED AMBASSADOR.

THE leader of the game, having prepared a number of little horns of paper that can be attached to the heads of the players—curl-paper fashion—commences by addressing to the person seated on his left in a circle the discourse which all the players must repeat after him word for word, without the slightest alteration or addition, on pain of receiving the name of *Horned Ambassador*, instead of that of *Royal Ambassador*, which all hold in right of the game. The speech is as follows :—

"Good morning, Royal Ambassador—always Royal. I, the Royal Ambassador—always Royal—come from his Royal Majesty—always Royal (indicating his neighbour on the right) to tell you that his eagle has a golden beak."

The second and following players repeat this formula as we have already stated. If any one makes a mistake, he receives one of the paper horns for each blunder. And in the following round, instead of saying, "I, the *Royal* Ambassador—always *Royal*" he says,—"I the *one* (two or three, according to the number he has received) *horned* Ambassador—*always horned*," &c.

By the same rule, when addressing the wearer of one or more horns, instead of saying, "Good day, *Royal* Ambassador—always *Royal*," it is necessary to say, "Good day, *one* (or more) *horned* Ambassador—always *horned*."

At the second round, the leader adds, and the others repeat successively, a new quality, to that mentioned as possessed by the king's eagle in the first—such as *brazen claws ;* 'at the third, *diamond eyes ;* at the fourth, *silver plumes ;* at the fifth, *an iron heart,* &c. The last act of this game (which may be prolonged *ad libitum*) is the collection of forfeits in proportion to the number of horns that have been distributed, and the penalties exacted for their redemption by the king of the *Ambassadors*—always *Royal*—from their many horned brethren.

CROSS PURPOSES.

THIS game is a decided improvement on *conversation cards,* as giving employment to a larger number of players, and being less troublesome in preparation.

Each player furnishes his neighbour with an *answer,* after the fashion of the *hidden word.** One of the party stands at a little distance, so as not to overhear what is said.

The office of this isolated individual (all the answers being arranged) is to come forward and address a question in turn to each player, who is bound to give the answer that has been confided to him by his neighbour. The result is often highly amusing.

This game offers no difficulty whatever, beyond that of

* Pages 83, 115.

knowing how to put the questions so as to make them apply to all sorts of answers.

Let us suppose that the members of a select company have been provided with an answer each, and that the interrogator (Charles) questions them, as follows :—

CHARLES. How do you find yourself to-day?

MARIA. With pepper and vinegar.

CHARLES. Are you fond of dancing?

ELLEN. On the table.

CHARLES. Are you fond of equestrian exercise?

ALEXANDER. Trimmed with point lace.

CHARLES. What is your opinion of Tennyson?

LUCY. Hot with sugar, &c. &c.

THE BOOK OF FATE.

THE president of the game takes a pack of cards, two or three of which he distributes to each player, reserving to himself the remainder, which he is at liberty to consult when necessary,—he having nothing to do with the game beyond his office of superintendent. Each player conceals his cards carefully from his neighbour.

The distribution concluded, the president asks the nearest player,—

"Have you read the Book of Fate?"

The player answers,—

" I have read the Book of Fate.

" What did you read in the Book of Fate ?"

"I read—so and so—" (naming whatever card he pleases, provided it be not one of those in his hand).

The president consults his reserve pack. If the card alluded to be in it, the player naming it pays a forfeit. If not, the others examine their cards, and the one in whose hand it is found, lays it on the table, and gives it to the president.

From this point, there are two methods of proceeding. One is, that if the person naming a card, and the one in whose hand it is found, be of different sexes, a kiss is exchanged between them ; if not, both pay forfeits. This, however, will subject the game to the restrictive conditions to be found in our note, page 20. The simpler, and wholly unobjectionable, method is, to make the holder of the card pay a forfeit, and acquit the namer of it.

In either case, the game continues ; that is to say, the player previously interrogated becomes questioner in his turn—inquiring of his neighbour on the left—" *Have you read, &c.*," and so on, till all the cards have returned to the hands of the president.

In the course of having to name so many cards, it is

enough that there should be some repetitions ; in case of which, the player so inattentive as to forget what have been already named, and to clash with the nomination of another, pays a forfeit. In consequence of this, and to avoid endless disputes, the president should take care to keep apart, from the rest of the pack, the cards already named ; to conceal them from the players, so as to give no hint of what has gone before ; and to consult them every time a fresh card is named.

It must also be rigidly observed, that any card named, and found in the hands of the speaker, costs him a forfeit for his negligence or stupidity. As the cards become exhausted, the players who have been relieved of theirs retire from the game. Those must refrain from giving any advice to the others, on pain of forfeit.

THE BUTTERFLY.

This is a game we have met with in the French work, so often gratefully mentioned in these pages. The writer introduces it with the following remark :—

" A fine and delicate gallantry may render this game very agreeable to the ladies invited to participate in it ; and the malice of their responses contribute not indifferently to augment the charm of it."

Recommending the gentlemen who have any idea of playing it to look up their stock of "fine and delicate gallantry," and the ladies on no account to fail in augmenting the charm by the necessary amount of "malice," we will proceed to the description of the game.

All the gentlemen assume the characters of garden insects, such as the *Butterfly* (who gives his name to, and leads off the game) the *Ant*, the *Wasp*, the *Beetle*, the *Bee*, the *Caterpillar*,* &c. &c.

The ladies represent different flowers†—the *Rose*, the *Honeysuckle*, the *Eglantine*, the *Geranium*, the *Violet*, &c. &c.

The names being distributed and understood, the Butterfly, as first speaker, commences talking about what he pleases. It must be borne in mind that no one must pronounce a name either of an insect or a flower that has not been adopted ; and that each player must take up the discourse as soon as the last speaker has pronounced his or her name, which he generally does, fixing his eyes on quite another person, so as to mislead the real bearer of it.

A name cited by mistake—the speech taken up too soon or too late—these are serious offences, to be punished in

---

* The Daddy-long-legs. (*Marginal note by a young gentleman who looked over our MS. without our permission*).

† "How nice!" (*Marginal note by a young lady who looked over our MS. at our especial request*).

the usual manner. It must also be observed, that the *insects* can only cite the names of *flowers*, and *vice versa*.

Specimen.

THE BUTTERFLY (*loquitor*). How embarrassing, to be sure, for a poor insect like myself to drop suddenly upon a garden glowing with the loveliest flowers, each one as beautiful as the other! How am I to make my choice? Now allured by the delicious perfumes, breathing from the half-opened lips of the budding *rose*—

THE ROSE. Hold your tongue! miserable insect! I have not forgotten that, yesterday, your envenomed kisses caused the death of the loveliest of my sisters? I would rather the meanest *ant*—

THE ANT. Say you so, beautiful flower? Since I have your permission, I will climb even to the top of your precious calyx before the *sun** has achieved one half of his course. I will there seek shelter when the *gardener** shall arrive armed with his *watering-pot** to add new bril-

* It is advisable to introduce now and then the three words—*sun, flower-pot,* and *gardener*. These for which the players are less prepared than the names of *flowers* and *insects,* usually produce a great many forfeits. The following are the by-laws with reference to the subject. At the mention of the *sun,* all should rise from their seats; at the *gardener,* all the flowers hold out their hands as if asking his assistance; and the *insects,* frightened, make a gesture as if they would shun his presence. Finally,

liancies to your beauty. I was up to this moment content with offering my homage to a simple *violet*—

THE VIOLET. At last then, I may enjoy a moment's repose. In vain I strove to conceal my leaves among the grass,—this contemptible insect has persecuted me as cruelly as the noisiest and fiercest *bee*—

THE BEE then takes up the word, and the game continues.

We question whether this game will ever become popular in America. As it is, however, rather our business to provide than to criticise, and as we did not catch the butterfly with the iutention of cruelly pulling him to pieces, we leave him in the hands of our readers,—trusting to their discernment to find out any beauties he may possess.

when the *watering-pot* is mentioned, all the *flowers* start up to their feet suddenly as if reanimated by the freshness of the water, and the *insects* fall each on one knee, as if prostrated by the same effect. These different postures only cease when the speaker has mer tioned the name of a flower or an insect, who in turn, takes up the wor l.

III. CATCH GAMES.

DEPENDING ON THE ASSISTANCE OF AN ACCOMPLICE, OR SECRET KNOWLEDGE FOR THE PURPOSE OF MYSTIFICATION.

THE WITCH.

A TRICK to discover a given word by the assistance of a confederate, who enacts the *witch*. Having entered the room, and taken your seat, you are addressed by his witch (who makes mystic passes, &c., over you with a wand) in different sentences, each commencing with a consonant in the word, in rotation. These sentences she divides by waving her wand over your head. The vowels are expressed by thumps on the floor with her wand—thus: a single thump for A ; two for E ; three for I ; four for O ; and five for U.

Example.

The word chosen is *Boatman*. The witch commences ;— " *B*-e prepared, my trusty spirit, to answer my questions.

(*Thump, thump, thump !—a wave of the wand—thump !*
T-o answer my questions, O spirit, so mind—(*a wave of*
the wand) *M*-ind what you are about (*thump*). *N*-ow ex-
pound the oracle."

The mystification of the audience may be increased by
fixing on the second or third letter instead of the first.

THE WIZARD.

THE wizard, as may be supposed, is a near relation of the
witch. In this, however, you do not profess to name the
article fixed on without having heard it, but simply to
detect which it is when named amongst others.

The secret is this : your confederate takes care to name
it after an object having *four legs*, as a quadruped or an
article of furniture.

Example.

The word agreed on is *lamp*. The confederate commences his interrogation :

  Q. Is it a flower ?
  A. No.
  Q. Is it an inkstand ?
  A. No

Q. Is it a table-cloth?

A. No.

Q. Is it a *table*?

A. No.

Q. Is it a LAMP?

A. Yes.

A table having four legs, the word following it is known to be the right one.

THE WHISTLE.

A WHISTLE is attached to the skirts of an unsuspecting individual. He is then placed in the middle of the players (all standing up) having been previously shown another whistle, which he is told is to be passed round the company, and sounded while his back is turned—his office being to detect the player. The person on whom he has turned his back adroitly takes hold of the whistle attached to him, and blows on it. The victim turns round quickly at the noise. The other, no less quick, has let go the whistle, and—while he is watching closely to detect its presence in this quarter—he hears it sounded at his back. He turns round again—whenever he looks for the whistle it is sounded behind him. It is as well to put a stop to the game at the first signs of insanity exhibited by the bewildered victim. This, however, is quite optional.

THE KING AND HIS SLAVE.

A KING* is chosen, and conducted with much pomp to a throne at one end of the room. Though elected by popular acclamation, this monarch is vested with powers scarcely less absolute than those of an hereditary despot.

The first act of his reign is to make a slave of one of his subjects. He fixes upon any one he likes. The slave submits—he had better! and is requested to seat himself at the foot of the throne.

The king then calls on one of the company by name, "——, approach, my subject."

If the player called upon be unacquainted with the etiquette of this powerful court, he will in all probability approach the presence rudely and without ceremony. He immediately pays a heavy forfeit into the royal treasury, and takes the place of the slave. This terrible punishment is inflicted, without the culprit being told the nature

* Or Queen.

of his offence.   As we have already said, the monarch is absolute and irresponsible.

If, on the contrary, the subject honoured by the royal summons should happen to know his duty, he says,—

" Sire, may I dare ?"

The king is graciously pleased to reply, " You may."

The subject then approaches, and says,—

" Sire, I have obeyed ; I await your royal orders,"

The king then orders him to take from the *slave* any ornament or superfluous article of dress he may think fit. But the subject (under the same penalties as before) must not proceed to execute the royal command without pronouncing the *formula*, " Sire, may I dare ?" to which the king, with the same enormous amount of condescension, again replies, " You may."

After the execution of the edict, the player repeats—

" Sire, I have obeyed ; I await your royal orders."

The king either commands him to take something else from the slave, or says, " Return to your place."   This, however, the player must take care not to do *at once*, on pain of taking the slave's place, and paying a forfeit. He must first say, " Sire, may I dare ?" as usual ; and not think of quitting the presence until the king says, " You may."

The articles taken from the slave are claimed by the state as forfeits,   It is seldom, however, he is stripped of

many of his ornaments.   This spoiler is almost sure to
neglect the necessary formula, previous to executing one
or other of the royal commands, and become an object for
plunder himself.

The king is elected for an unlimited period, but may
abdicate whenever he pleases, with the privilege of ap-
pointing his successor.   With all his absolute power, he
had, however, better take care.   We have seen unpopular,
partial, and especially stupid monarchs dethroned at a
moment's notice.

THE COOK WHO DOESN'T LIKE PEAS.

THE leader of the game puts the following question to
the assembled players in succession :—

" My cook doesn't like peas ; what shall we give her to
eat ?"

A player suggests " turnips," " potatoes," " a piece of
bread," " chops," " a penny roll," " pork," &c.

To all these, the questioner replies, " She doesn't like
them (or it)—pay a forfeit."

Another proposes " carrots," " dry bread," " beef,"
" mutton," &c., the answer to any of which is,—

" That will suit her," and the *questioner* pays a forfeit.

THE CLAIRVOYANT

If only two or three are in the secret, the game proceeds for some time to the intense mystification of the players, who have no idea what they have said to incur or escape the penalties. It depends upon a play of words. The cook not liking " *P's*," the players must avoid giving an answer in which that letter occurs. As the same proposition must not be repeated twice, those even who are in the plot are sometimes entrapped ; the answer they had resolved on being forestalled by another player ; they have no time for consideration.

THE CLAIRVOYANT BEHIND THE SCREEN.

A PLAYER from whom it is considered desirable to extract as many forfeits as possible, is placed behind a screen, or a door in an adjoining room. All the rest conceal themselves from his sight, and the conductor of the game cries out,

"We are ready, are you there ?"

"Yes."

"So let us begin. Do you know Miss Such-a-one" (naming one of the ladies of the company) ?

"Yes."

"Do you know how she is dressed ?"

"Yes."

"Do you know her gown?"

"Yes."

"Her bracelets?"

"Yes."

"Good.   Do you know her sleeves ; the lace on her scarf?"

"Yes."

"Her chatelaine ; her watch?"

"Yes."

"*And* her watch chain?"

"Yes."

"In fact you know all her external decorations?"

"Yes."

"Her gloves ; her bouquet?"

"Yes."

The questioner adds as many objects, and varies his inquiries as often as he pleases. The other replies "Yes," invariably.

"Well, as you know so much about it, tell me by which of the articles I have mentioned, I now take hold of her."

If the clairvoyant be not *au fait* to the game, he will, doubtless, name an iufinity of things before hitting on the right one, and will pay a forfeit for each mistake. He also pays one in case of his naming an article not previously mentioned by the questioner.

If acquainted with the secret of the game, he would say (the questions above given having been put to him),

"You have hold of Miss ——— by her *watch-chain*"— that being the sole article to which the questioner had prefixed the conjunction *and*—the word of recognition for the initiated clairvoyant.

When the object is to victimize any particular individual (always a laudable one in any case) in this manner, the plan is to fix on two or three clairvoyants, in the secret, to precede him. These, of course, pretend to be mistaken a few times to evade suspicion. When the last of them has guessed correctly (as he might have done at once had he wished), the clairvoyant being entitled to nominate his successor, he fixes on the innocent lamb doomed, from the commencement, to sacrifice.

THE SCISSORS.

A PAIR of scissors, or any other object to represent one, is passed from hand to hand—each player saying as he presents it to his neighbour, "I make you a present of my scissors, open or shut" (as he may choose).

In the first case the player must cross either his arms

or legs carelessly, so as not to attract attention; in the second he must take care to keep them separate.

Many people from the want of attention, are made to pay forfeits for a long time without knowing why, their surprise and perplexity being the chief amusement of the game.

THE MOLE IN THE FARMER'S FIELD.

ONE player addresses another :—" Have you seen the mole in the farmer's field ?"

The other replies,—

" Yes, I have seen the mole in the farmer's field."

" Do you know what the mole does ?"

" Yes, I know what the mole does."

" Can you do as he does ?"

The secret is to *shut your eyes* every time you answer (all the answers being echoes of the questions in the affirmative). Failing in this, you pay a forfeit.

I'VE BEEN TO MARKET.

THE company being formed into a circle, one of the players says to his neighbour on the left,—

"I've been to market."

The neighbour inquires—

"What have you bought?"

"A coat, a dress, a nosegay, a shoe:" in fact anything that may come into the head of the *customer*, provided he be able, on pronouncing the word, to *touch* an article such as he has named. Whoever neglects or is unable to perform this ceremony pays a forfeit. Naming an article previously indicated is similarly punished.

HOT COCKLES FOR TWO.

THIS game is executed *apparently* in the same manner as *Hot Cockles*, only that there are two *confessors*, who receive on their laps the heads of two patients. One of these must be acquainted with the trick of the game; the other without the slightest suspicion of it. The former, (when both have concealed their faces,) quietly gets up, and strikes the hand of his companion with his own; then returns to his place, and appears to rise at the same time as the other.

It will be believed that the victim may go on guessing for ever, without hitting upon the right person. The other, at the end of a few turns, names, according to his own choice, any member of the company, who immediately affects to be detected fairly, and takes his place. This is done to avoid awakening suspicions. The game is continued till the victim gives it up in despair, and declares himself at the mercy of the company, who ruin him in forfeits for his want of perception.

V. GAMES.

REQUIRING THE EXERCISE OF FANCY, INTELLIGENCE, EVEN IMMAGINATION.

THE STOOL OF REPENTANCE;

OR, THE COURT OF JUSTICE.

ONE of the party, by lots, or his own choice, is fixed upon to occupy the Stool of Repentance, as culprit. Another takes the office of President of the Court. The remainder form the judges.

The legal proceedings are commenced by the President in the following manner :—pointing to the culprit, he inquires of the judges—

"My lords, do you know why the prisoner, J——, has been sentenced to solitary confinement on the Stool of Repentance ?"*

The judges answer—" We do."

---

* We are not answerable for this startling Law Reform which makes the court sit in judgment on a culprit after sentence has been carried out.

They then advance, one by one, and whisper, in the President's ear, whatever reasons they may think fit to give, consisting of the most ridiculous accusations against the prisoner.

All the depositions being made, they resume their places, and the President addresses the culprit :—

"Prisoner on the Stool, you are accused of"—(here he repeats the various accusations). "Can you tell me who it is that has brought forward these serious charges against you ?"

The prisoner then repeats all the charges ; naming, to each, the particular judge he suspects of having made it. If he should fail in fixing any one upon the right person, he pays a forfeit for each mistake, and continues to occupy the stool, that he may meet a fresh ground of accusations. Should he name one correctly, the detected judge, whoever it may be, pays a forfeit, and occupies the stool of repentance in his place. Proceedings are immediately commenced against the newly-caught prisoner.

Simple as this game appears, it cannot be thoroughly enjoyed without the exercise of three important qualities— memory, sprightliness, and delicacy. The first is necessary to the President, who has to receive the various accusations from the judges, and remember them distinctly, so as to be able to identify each with its author when the guessing on the part of the culprit commences: the se-

cond and third to the judges—one to enable them to in-
vent charges of an appropriate and amusing character,
the other in order that those charges may be so constructed as to avoid all possibility of wounding the feelings of
the culprit.

With regard to the latter necessity, we cannot do better than to quote a little French work (to which we have
been greatly indebted in the course of our labours on
various occasions) on the subject.*

"This game requires great attention on the part of the accusing
judges. They have to consider the age, the sex, the physical and mental
qualities of the person before them on the stool of repentance (*sellette*).
When the object is to pay him a compliment, care should be taken to
avoid citing a quality not possessed by him, or of which the possession
by him is exaggerated, the mention of which would be construed into
unpleasant irony. If it be a question of a fault or ridiculous quality, it
were much better to make the accusation entirely fictitious than to base
it upon an actual failing, any allusion to which would convey an impression of ill-breeding. As a rule it is as well to avoid excess in all cases,
and to observe scrupulously the decencies of society, the forgetfulness of
which often leads to ill feeling, in games of play, as in all other social
relations."

The homely good sense of this exhortation is too obvious to need the slightest comment.

* *Almanach des Jeux de Société*, 1853.

ACTING RHYMES.

A WORD is fixed upon to which all the players in succession have to express a rhyme in dumb show.

Example.

We will suppose the given word to be *root*.

The first player elevates his leg, tugging at the air, and making faces of pain, as if undergoing the agony of pulling on a tight *boot*.

The second points an imaginary gun to *shoot*.

The third looks sentimentally up at a picture-frame, as to a lady's casement, and, assuming the aspect of a despondent lover, appears to be playing the *lute*.

The fourth makes violent and angry faces, thumping his palm as if in the height of a *dispute*.

The fifth turns his shirt-collar down, rocks his chair back, puts his heels on the mantelpiece in American fashion, " whittles" the arm of his chair with a knife, and winks knowingly, with his finger to his nose, by way of indicating that he is *'cute*.

The sixth twists up a roll of paper, and puts it up to his mouth, making the grimaces usually attendant on the early studies of the *flute*, &c. &c.

Forfeits may be exacted for imperfect or badly-expressed rhymes.

The amusement of the game, of course, depends on the nature of the rhymes selected by the players, and their powers of expressing them humourously.

THE SECRETARY.

THIS game, for which—in company with many others in this collection, not to mention numerous original five-act comedies and three-volume novels—we are indebted to the French—may be played after two methods.

For either, it is necessary that the players should seat themselves round a table, provided with a sufficient number of pens, inkstands—in fact, as they say in the early copies of the original English comedies we have alluded to—*tout-ce qu'il faut pour écrire.*

The *Secretary* (so the presiding genius of the game is called) distributes to each a blank piece of paper.

Supposing the old manner of playing the game to be the one decided on ; each player writes his name distinctly at the top of his piece of paper—which he hands back to the Secretary. The Secretary shuffles (as the secretaries of more important societies *will* do sometimes) the papers, and then distributes them at random among the players—each being ignorant of the name that has fallen to the lot of his neighbour. Each player then, and without the slightest constraint or reserve, writes under the name he has got hold of, what he thinks of the person bearing it ; folds up his production, and hands the paper a second time to the Secretary, who, having received all the contributions, shuffles them once more, and then reads aloud the various criticisms—without permitting any one to inspect the handwritings.

We confess that we never played at this game (a thing we can say of few games of the kind—English or French), but we fancy a good deal of fun might be got out of it ; and cannot see any danger in its being pursued by people who know how to conduct themselves.

With our thin-skinned neighbours across the Atlantic, however, the case appears to be different. Our authority* informs us, that at the conclusion of the reading it is necessary to adopt the most stringent measures ;

"All the papers are thrown into the fire, in order to avoid the quarrels that the malicious insinuations contained in them might give rise to, if the authors were known."

Even this regulation does not seem to have placed things on a safe footing. We are told that—

* The *Almanach des Jeux de Société*, already alluded to.

"As this game frequently degenerates into personalities—dangerous from their results—a new method has been invented, not subject to the same inconveniences."

The new method is certainly safe enough—even we should think, for Frenchmen.   It is as follows :—

When the Secretary has distributed his bits of paper, each player assumes any name he thinks proper—as applicable to his character or to any qualities with which he may choose to invest himself, which he writes down after his real name, without letting his neighbours see the name he has adopted.   This done, the Secretary collects all the names, and makes all possible haste to write out upon a similar number of pieces of paper, the adopted name of any one person he may think fit to select.   These he distributes among the players, each of whom—in a state of frenzy to find out the person to whom the name belongs—writes a fancy sketch of character, which he signs with his own adopted name.   In this manner, says the authority already quoted,

"You frequently eulogise a person you would not have cared to compliment had you known whom you were addressing,—or literally pull to pieces another to whom you would have wished to say something agreeable.   From this results a series of *quid-pro-quos*, all the more amusing from the fact that the Secretary having read aloud all the criticisms, tears away the mask from each writer, and no one has the right to feel annoyed at the affront, or flattered at the compliments, accidentally heaped upon him."

Albeit we admit the new method to be an amusing
variety, we must own to a preference for the old one,—
which we cannot regard in any other light than a harm-
less opportunity for good humoured quizzing. We can
only thank our neighbours, the French, for inventing
delightful games for us—regretting that their "touchy"
dispositions should prevent their participation in our en-
joyment of them.

THE GAME OF DEFINITIONS.

MANY of our readers will remember a delightful little
work by Mr. Wallbridge Lunn, published a few years ago,
entitled " *The Council of Four, or a game of definitions.*"
This purported to be the result of certain spare evenings
hanging on the hands of four friends, who, finding nothing
else to do, amused themselves in the following manner :—
A word was given, of which each of the party wrote
an epigrammatic definition,—all four being given in
anonymously, and subsequently read aloud.
The uniform excellence of the published definitions
has led to the suspicion, that Mr. Lunn himself was the
author of them all ;—in fact that, to quote Mrs. Mala-
prop, he was like Mr. Cerberus (beating that individual,

it should be observed, by a head), "*four* gentlemen at once." Be this as it may, his unobtrusive little book has suggested a means of passing away a very agreeable hour; for which we, for one among many, have often had occasion to feel grateful.

We should remark, that this being purely an intellectual exercise, and depending entirely upon the interchange of thought, should not be attempted in a hazardously mixed company. It should only be proposed among friends of certain elevated and even literary tastes, well acquainted with each others capabilities. To all such we unhesitatingly recommend it.

The following specimens, strung together at random, are our recollections of the game as played on various occasions :—

ELECTRICITY.

Fettered lightning.

The musician of the spheres who beats Time.

PARLIAMENT.

The national kitchen, where everything that's good goes to the cook's cousin.

The waiting-room of the Opera.

GAS.

The evening edition of the Sun.

A regular flare-up, given by Old King Coal.

BLOOMERISM.

A preliminary to shaving the ladies.

STEAM.

A daring highwayman—stopping all the mail coaches.
The surgeon's *vade mecum*.
The world's hare—the telegraph's tortoise.

PROVERBS.

ONE of the party is sent out of the room.: the rest busy-
ing themselves with thinking of a proverb, a poetical
quotation, or any known sentence—to be discovered by
him on his return.

To effect this, he is entitled to ask questions from the
company all round, beginning with the person on his left.
The question may be whatever he pleases, but the answer
from the first person must contain the first word of the
proverb; from the second, the second; and so on, each
player taking a word in succession, going round the company as many times as may be necessary, till the proverb
be completed.

The great skill of the game is to contrive the answers
so that the fatal word may not be conspicuous,

Example.

The proverb chosen is, " *A bird in the hand is worth two in the bush.*"

QUESTION, No. 1.   What do you think of the weather ?

ANSWER.   I think it will be A fine day to-morrow.

Q. No. 2.   Hum !   What do you think—do you think we shall have rain ?

A.   I have no corns.   I am neither a jackass, a peacock, nor a barometer ; nor any BIRD, beast, or mathematical instrument, to indicate the weather.

Q. No. 3.   What is your opinion of the domestic policy of the Peruvians ?

A.   I think they behaved very well IN the matter of the Lobos Islands.

Q. No. 4.   What is the difference between fish alive and live fish ?

A.   THE difference there is between a cow and an oyster-knife.

Q. No. 5.   What is the opinion of Pythagoras respecting wild-fowl ?

A.   I have not a copy of Shakspeare at HAND at present.

Q. No. 6.   Do you think there is any prospect of a war between Jerusalem and Madagascar ?

A.   I am inclined to think there *is.*

Q. No. 7.   If a herring and a half costs three cents,
what is the price of mackerel in the height of the season?

A.   The question is not WORTH answering.

Q. No. 7.   Do you think I shall solve this difficult
problem?

A.   Probably, in the year Nineteen hundred and fifty-
TWO.

Q. No. 9.   Come, you'll help me to find it out, won't
you?

A.   Not if it's IN my power to avoid so doing.

Q. No. 10.   Do you feel inclined to work me a pair
of braces?

A.   Not in THE least, I assure you.   You don't de-
serve it.

Q. No. 11.   Can't you do anything to assist me in my
experiments?

A.   I am not to be caught with salt.   I know how
many beans make five.   I object to beating about the
BUSH; and you may catch a weasel asleep, if you have
the power.

The player may make his answer as long as he likes,
but must be able to repeat it word for word, if called
upon to do so.   In the example we have given, the word
bush (however artfully overlaid) would probably lead to
detection, from the rarity of its occurrence in ordinary

conversation, and the well-known character of the proverb. It is therefore advisable to select proverbs or quotations composed of the most ordinary phrases. The guesser may be allowed some time for deliberation ; but if compelled to give it up finally, must leave the room again and try another.

HOW, WHEN, AND WHERE.

THIS, like *Proverbs, Magic, Music,* &c., is a trial of skill between one player and all the rest ; on his side to discover a secret,—on theirs to prevent or render difficult its discovery. In this case he has to find out a word (the name of some article) they have thought of during his absence, by asking all round, three questions :—

"How do you like it ?"
"When do you like it ?"
"Where do you like it ?"

—to all of which, they are compelled to give reasonable answers, with the privilege (and of course the object) of leading the questioner as far astray as possible.

Example.

There are eight players (exclusive of the questioner). The word agreed upon is *box.*

The first question,—" *How do you like it ?*" is put to the players all round. The following answers are elicited by it in succession :—

1. Lined with satin.
2. Strong.
3. Gentle.
4. Made of Gold.
5. With a pretty girl in it.
6. Full of jewels.
7. With stabling for two or three ponies.
8. About a foot high.

To the second question,—" *When do you like it ?*"

1. When I want to keep awake.
2. In December.
3. In June.
4. In September.
5. When there's anything worth seeing.
6. When I'm travelling.
7. On Thursdays.
8. When I have not to open it just before bedtime.

To the third question,—" *Where do you like it ?*"

1. In the Highlands.
2. In my waistcoat pocket.
3. At Castle Garden.
4. On the lawn.
5. In my purse.

6. On anybody else's head but my own.

7. Behind four horses.

8. Opposite the Crystal Palace.

It will be seen that the various definitions of *Box*—*Christmas box, Coach box, Box on the ear, Box at the opera, Snuff box, Pill box, Box wood*, have been intended in the foregoing answers. It is always advisable to select a word capable of receiving as many meanings as possible.

If compelled to "give it up," the questioner is told what the word was, and punished for his stupidity by having to find out another. Should he succeed in guessing it, he changes places with one of his late adversaries, for whom a fresh word is fixed upon.

YES AND NO.

THIS game, which is of the same class as the preceding, was formerly called *Animal, Vegetable, and Mineral.* A player was sent out of the room, and a word (or rather thing) thought of. The player was called in, and proceeded to ask certain members of the company to which of the three kingdoms—*animal, vegetable,* or *mineral*—the object in question belonged. They were bound to tell him; and if composed of productions of two or more kingdoms, to give him full particulars. For instance, if the object were a *saddle*, in whose manufacture leather, wood, and metal are employed, he was told that it belonged to all three. He then proceeded to ask other questions, to which the players were only compelled to answer " Yes" or " No," as the case might be, and to take no notice whatever of questions not admitting of either of those very straightforward answers.

The game is now much simplified, being confined to the latter regulation. The guesser enters the room, and begins asking what questions he likes, the players only answering " Yes" and " No." He may ask if the article belongs to either of the three kingdoms, as well as any other question, and will receive a direct answer. But if its composition should belong to more than one (as in the case of the saddle) the player is not obliged to tell him unless directly questioned.

We will give our readers a specimen of how this game is carried on, and of the method in which the detection of the most out-of-the-way objects is usually arrived at.

We will suppose the article thought of to be *the lightning conductor on Barnum's Museum*,—a thing it would seem almost impossible to hit upon, without any clue beyond that afforded by the rules of the game.

The questioner begins by asking if it is animal.

" No."

"Is it vegetable?"

"No."

"Is it mineral?"

"Yes."

Mineral! There is one important point gained.

"Is it a particular object?"

"Yes."

"I mean not merely a particular class or description of objects?"

"No."

Something more definite!

"Have I ever seen it?"

"Yes."

"Is it in this house?"

"No."

"Is it in New York?"

"Yes."

"In the city?"

"No."

"In the west end?"

"Yes."

"In a house?"

"No."

"In a street?"

"No."

"In a public place?"

"Yes."

"In one of the parks or squares?"

"No."

He is a little at fault. The knowledge of the locality, however, is a great thing for him to hold on by. He continues :—

"Is it in the most fashionable part of the west end?"

"No."

"Near Broadway?"

"Yes."

"Top?"

"No."

"Bottom?"

"Yes."

The whereabouts being now so nearly ascertained, he returns to the nature of the article.

"Mineral, you say; is it metal?"

"Yes."

"A precious metal?"

"No."

"Iron?"

"Yes."

"Iron! and in a public place; neither in a house, a street, a park, or a square. Near the bottom of Broadway."

He is now so clearly on the scent that it is needless to

accompany him further. It will be seen that a system of first generalizing, then gradually centralizing the various heads of information, is the one to be pursued.

ACTING PROVERBS.

THIS is a more complicated version of the *Rhymes*. Each player must represent, by dumb show, a proverb, or well-known quotation or saying, in a sufficiently intelligible manner to enable at least one of the company to repeat it aloud. As, however, the performance may sometimes happen to be too obscure for the highest capacity, a president should be elected—(well up in the game)—empowered to demand an explanation of the actor's intentions from himself, when the riddle has been given up by the entire company, and to put it to the vote whether such explanation shall be admitted or not.

In case of its being pronounced satisfactory, the audience pay forfeits for their dulness of perception in not finding out the proverb. In case of its rejection, the performer pays one, as the penalty for his inability to render himself intelligible.

Examples.

PROVERB No. I.—The performer takes something to

represent a large stone, and rolls it for a considerable distance. He then picks it up, looks at it as if expecting to find something on it, and appears disappointed. He rolls it again, picks it up again and shows it to the company, appearing (by appropriate action) to think its nakedness a singular phenomenon.

The explanation of this proverb will soon be given.—"A rolling stone gathers no moss."

No. II.—A gentleman tries to make himself up for the character of a male bird of the barn-door species as nearly as possible. He opens the performance by appearing to be at roost, with his head tucked under the side of his wing and one leg in the air. Gradually he awakens and appears to be snuffing the morning air. He crows; but, not being thoroughly awake, drops off again. He awakens a second time, shaking his imaginary feathers and crowing prodigiously, as if it were really time to rouse himself. He does so, and indicates as well as may be that he wants his breakfast. He seeks for it on the ground for some time, but without success. At length he sees something. He flaps his wings with delight, and stoops to pick the article up with his beak. He secures and swallows it up with much *gusto*, and crows repeatedly by way of expressing his delight and assisting digestion.

Explanation.—"It's the early bird that picks up the worm."

No. III.—The player represents (as well as he can) a barber, who appears anxious to operate on something with the razor which he is supposed to brandish in his hand. He gives an imitation of the grunting of a pig.* He approaches the suppositious animal—lathers and shaves it—the pig appearing to make great vocal and muscular resistance. The barber looks at his razor and is in despair at finding nothing on it.

Explanation.—" Much cry and little wool—as the barber said when he shaved the pig."

No. IV.—The performer assumes the interesting peculiarities of an infant of tender years, just able to walk alone. The dear child, anxious for a little innocent amusement, takes hold of the poker by the wrong end—screams as having burnt its dear little hand, and dances round the room in agony. The blessed infant, on once more coming near the fireplace, starts back in terror, and, appearing to recollect that its misfortunes came from that quarter, runs away howling.

Explanation.—" A burnt child dreads the fire."

THE HIDDEN WORD.

EACH player whispers in the ear of his neighbour (on

* Inarticulate sounds of this description are admitted. Human speech only is prohibited.

the right) a word—whatever one he pleases ; but, in order
to make the game more interesting, it is advisable that
this should be of an out-of-the-way and marked description. The advantages of this will soon be obvious.

When every one knows his word (which he must keep
to himself), the player who gave the first word turns
round and commences the game by asking a question of
his neighbour on the *left*, who is obliged in his reply to
introduce the word given to him by his neighbour. This
he must do (on the principle of the *Proverbs**) so adroitly
as to prevent the questioner's detecting it from the words
by which it is surrounded.

Example.

We will suppose the word given to be *Mackintosh* ;
and that the questioner asks—

" Are you fond of poetry?"

There is as little connexion between poetry and a mackintosh as between any two articles we can think of.
The answer, however, may be constructed as follows :—

" I love poetry with all my soul ; but, in this bustling
age of steam, factories, electricity, *Mackintosh* and gutta
percha, I fear the voice of the Muse has little chance of
making itself heard."

If the questioner does not detect the word at once

* See page 113.

(two attempts not being allowed) he pays a forfeit. If he guesses correctly, the other pays, as a punishment for not having sufficiently bewildered his interrogator.

COMPLIMENTS.

PLAYING at compliments may justly be considered a very old game indeed. The following, however, is a new form of that popular species of entertainment.

A circle is formed of ladies and gentlemen placed alternately. Politeness demands that a lady should commence the game; politeness also demands that the lady may be allowed to let it alone if she likes; so that the regulation is immaterial.

However, supposing a lady does commence, she does it by saying,—

" I should like to be such or such an animal" (the more ridiculous or disagreeable the animal, the more difficult will be the compliment she is entitled to expect—founded on her wish).

We will suppose, for example, she has fixed upon a *black-beetle*. She asks of her neighbour on the left, what reason she could have had for wishing to be anything so absurd.

The neighbour on the left, who is *not expected to pay her a compliment,* replies, " because she has a taste for the kitchen ;" " because she likes treacle," or whatever he pleases.

The lady then turns to her neighbour *on the right,* and asks him the same question.

Neighbour No. 2 replies gallantly, " That you might lose all traces of your present beauty, which, from the mischief it does, your tender heart looks upon it in the light of a calamity."

If No. 1 has said what may be construed into a compliment, and No. 2 what cannot, both pay forfeits.

It is now the turn of No. 2 (the payer of the compliment *or* the forfeit) to express a wish. He says, for example, that he would like to be a *goose,* and asks the lady whom he has just complimented, why she thinks he would like to be that (except under apple-sauce circumstances) contemptible bird.

The lady, unmindful of his recent civility, ungratefully replies, " Because you are perfectly satisfied with yourself, and have no wish to change your condition." He then seeks a more flattering explanation of his motives from the lady on his right, who replies, " Because the dearest hope of your heart is to save your country, as the geese did in the Capitol of Rome."

Once round is quite enough for this game, which would

soon become fatiguing. It is right, though, to finish the round, if only for the sake of giving every player a chance of hearing something civil said to him, which he may not often meet with.

THE BOUQUET.

EACH player composes in his turn a bouquet of three different flowers which he names aloud to the conductor of the game.

The conductor writes down the names of the flowers, adding to each the name of a person in the company,— saying nothing to anybody of such addition. He then inquires of the supposed manufacturer of the bouquet what he intends doing with the flowers he has chosen. The player announces his intentions, whatever they may be, and the conductor applies them to the three persons whose names he has written.

Example.

The CONDUCTOR. Miss Arabella, have the kindness to choose three flowers.

ARABELLA. The rose, the dahlia, and the camelia.

CONDUCTOR. I have taken note of them carefully. Now tell me what you mean to do with the rose?

ARABELLA. I will put it in water.

CONDUCTOR. And the Dahlia?

ARABELLA. I will throw it out of the window.

CONDUCTOR. And the Camelia?

ARABELLA. I will wear it in my waistband till it dies.

CONDUCTOR. Good. You have put Mr. Jenkins in water, thrown Mrs. Thompson out of the window, and must wear Mr. Heavysides in your waistband till he dies. Now Mr. Walker, you have the kindness, &c. &c.

THE BOUQUET INTERPRETED.

THIS is a method of paying a compliment, or the reverse, by means of the Language of Flowers. The player, having intentions either way, selects three flowers of various meanings applying to the individual for whom they are designed, ties them round with a string, and appears to place them in a vase, for which he improvises an appropriate inscription. Lastly, the bouquet is presented to the person for whom it was intended.

Examples.

A young lady fatigued with the importunate attentions of a disagreeable young gentleman, or pretending to be so with a young gentleman whom she adopts this method of assuring she does not consider at all disagreeable (such inexplicable means, we are assured, being sometimes resorted to), expresses herself as follows :—

"I choose a *poppy*, an *Indian pink*, and a *thistle*.

"The *poppy* is the emblem of weariness leading to sleep ; the *Indian pink* of false pride ; and the *thistle* the most appropriate present that can be given to a certain species of quadrupeds,

"I tie up my bouquet with a halter.

"I place it in a leaden vase, on which I inscribe, ' Give every man his deserts, and who shall escape whipping ?'

"Finally, I present the whole to Mr. Swellington, who need not trouble himself to thank me."

A young man, under certain despondent circumstances, would rush at the opportunity of at last making himself understood in the following impassioned manner :—

"I select a *rose*, a *pansy*, and a *lily of the valley*.

"The *rose* is the emblem of beauty : the *pansy*, while in one sense it means *thought*, and is the emblem of mind, in another expresses a *heart's ease* that should know no interruption : the *lily* is purity itself.

"I tie them up in a true lover's knot—symbol of my unyielding constancy.

"I place them in a vase of gold, on which I inscribe —' Sweets to the sweet ;' and I present them on my knees to Miss Swansdown."

TRANSFORMATIONS.

THIS game appears to have been founded on the *Stool of Repentance*,—than which it is scarcely less entertaining.

The player with the best number undertakes the office of Master of the Ceremonies.

All the members of the company are transformed in turns ; that is to say, they fix on some piece of furniture, or other article, which they say they would like to be. It is usual to commence the game with a lady.

We will suppose a lady has decided on a *mirror*. She says, "I should like to be a mirror." The master of the ceremonies then goes round the company and addresses to each player, in succession, the following questions :—

" If Miss So-and-so were a mirror, what would you do with her ? What would you think of her ? or what would you wish to be ?" The players' return to one or more of these questions whatever answers may suggest themselves ; whispered in the ear of the master of the ceremonies. When he has received them all, he advances to the transformed, and repeats them aloud to her ; her office being to identify their authors. As many as are found out, pay forfeits ; if none, it is the transformed who pays ; and a second transformation is proceeded with.

The *finesse* of this game consists in applying pointed and facetious observations to the character of the transformed,—having reference, also, to the article he has chosen to represent.

For instance, in the case already given of the mirror, allusions would be made to the lady's *brilliancy*, and strong *powers of reflection ;* one would like to hang her up in his room ; another would like to have his arms transformed into a golden frame for her, &c. &c.

Supposing a gentleman to represent a *sideboard*, he can be said to be *empty ; wooden ; hollow ; he wants to be trusted with the spirits ; he has an eye to the spoons and plate ; he is no ornament to any room, &c.*

With the exercise of a little humour and imagination it will be easy to form on these models *apropos* of a sufficiently amusing description.

THE SONG ON A GIVEN SUBJECT.

This is a condition seldom imposed, except on a lady or gentleman not only possessed of an agreeable voice— but also of some impromptu power—either of invention or application.

If the penitent be able to *extemporize* a song, so much the better ; but if not, he should endeavour to choose one from his collection, whose bearing on the subject given will be marked by some degree of taste and intelligence.

The alteration or parodying of an occasional name or passage, may be introduced with effect.

As a rule, a single verse will be found sufficient. If the song chosen should happen to contain more than one, it is always safe to stop at the conclusion of the first. If the audience require any more, you may rely upon their telling you so.

PROVERBS.

See the game *Proverbs in Action*, in this collection. The only difference is that, in this case, the acting is confined to the person condemned to perform one or more for the redemption of his forfeit.

THE WILL.

The player ordered to make his will, bequeaths to each of his companions something he possesses—either an article of property, or any moral or physical quality. This is, of course, an inexhaustible source of compliments or sarcasms; in dispensing the latter of which, however, we need scarcely advise our readers to use as much delicacy and discrimination as possible, so as to avoid inflicting a wound in a too susceptible quarter.

THE BOUQUET.

See the game bearing the same title; the act of penance is performed in the same manner, with the exception that it does not go round the company.

GOOD ADVICE.

The penitent gives—either in whispers or aloud, according to the order he has received—any piece of advice that may come into his head, to one or all of the company.

COMPARISONS.

You are ordered to compare a lady (or a gentleman) to some object or other—and explain in what respect she (or he) resembles that object, and in what differs from it.

For instance—a lady compares a gentleman to a sheet of white paper;

The resemblance exists in the facility with which both receive a first impression—the difference, in the promptness with which the gentleman alone can receive impressions in quick succession, one after another, which are as quickly effaced.

A gentleman compares a lady to a chimney clock;

Like that article of furniture, she ornaments the room wherein she is placed; but, unlike it, makes us forget the hours as they fly, instead of calling attention to them, &c.

THE EMBLEM.

Not differing from the comparisons, except that it is confined to the *resemblance* portion.

A gentleman suggests as the emblem of a certain lady

—let us say, a salamander. The lady asks him " Why?" ".Because," is the gallant reply, " you live unscathed in the midst of those fires which consume all who approach you."

A lady pronounces a well to be the emblem of a man of learning—not given to be communicative: " He is profound," she says, " but it is rather troublesome to draw out the good contained in him."

THE DOOR CHEEK.

The player (a gentleman, we will assume) condemned to this act of penance, stands up with his back against a door. Thus placed, he calls on a lady to come and stand face to face with him. The lady complies, and then calls upon a gentleman, who has to come and stand with his back to hers ; and so on with the whole of the company —care being taken that the last couple of the row be placed back to back. The row being complete, the *crier* of the forfeits gives a signal, at which every one turns round and kisses the person with whom he now finds himself face to face. The result is that the original penitent has nothing to kiss but the *door cheek*, on which he is bound to bestow a salute as tender as those whose echoing smacks reverberate behind him.

THE PRIVATE OPINION.

This act scarcely differs from that of *Good Advice*—

only that instead of sage counsels you impart (aloud or in whispers, as may be agreed on) to all the players your private opinion of them.

THE SECRET.

This consists in whispering a secret to each member of the company.

THE TELEGRAPHIC MESSAGE.

If ordered to send a message round the room, by Electric Telegraph, you arrange all the players in a circle, alternately composed of ladies and gentlemen. You then whisper whatever you like in the ear of your next neighbour, who repeats it to the next, and so on round the circle, till the message comes back to you. You are then compelled to declare aloud if it has been faithfully transmitted; and, if not, in what particulars it has been altered. Some alterations may generally be relied on, from the number of speakers the message has to be intrusted to, added to the *amour propre* of some who may feel touched in some tender point by its nature, and who will naturally be tempted to make some slight deviations.

THE CONFIDENTIAL ANSWER.

Founded on the principle of *Conversation Cards, Cross Purposes*, &c. The penitent places himself last in a row of three persons, the first of which whispers whatever he likes to the second. The penitent has heard nothing, but is obliged to whisper to the aforesaid second person an answer to the observation of the first. The "middle man" then repeats aloud what has been confided to him on either side. The result is generally an amusing species of cross-reading.

THE DECLARATION OF LOVE.

The penitent is ordered to make a declaration of love to a lady pointed out to him, or one he may fix upon of his own free will, in impromptu verse.

Example.

"If loving you be criminal, than I
Where lives the wretch more justly doomed to die?
Slay me at once, and further wrong prevent,
Since never of my crime can I repent."

In the dearth of invention, considerable latitude may be allowed in the matter of plagiarism from popular authors.

Example.

"If you loves me as I loves you,
No knife can cut our loves in two."

THE PERFECT WOMAN.

The player commanded to manufacture a perfect woman, selects from each lady present some particular charm of mind or person possessed by her. All these admirable qualities being combined in one imaginary individual, the necessary pitch of female excellence is supposed to be attained.

THE ACROSTIC.

This feat is a sort of appendix to the game entitled the *Alphabet*—in which the player says, " I love my love with an A, &c."

A lady inquires of the penitent why he loves *and* hates her with such or such a word. He replies by giving her a list of her good qualities, and also one of her imperfections, each list to form an *acrostic* on the given word.

Examples.

The gentleman is supposed to love and hate (we are not responsible for the contradictory nature of the proceeding) with RAPTURE.

The following good and bad qualities are offered in explanation :—

Good.	*Bad.*
The lady is ROSY.	She is RANCOROUS.
" AMIABLE.	" ARTFUL.
" PLEASING.	" PROUD.
" TENDER.	" TREACHEROUS.

The lady is UNSWERVING.   She is UGLY.†
   "   RICH.*   "   RUTHLESS.
   "   ELEGANT.   "   ENVIOUS.

The word given is DESPAIR.

She is DEVOTED.   She is DECEITFUL.
   "   ENLIGHTENED.   "   EXTRAVAGANT.
   "   SPRIGHTLY.   "   SLOVENLY.
   "   PENETRATING.   "   POOR (shame!)
   "   ARDENT.   "   ABSOLUTE.
   "   INCOMPARABLE.   "   IDLE.
   "   RARE.   "   RAPACIOUS.

THE THREE WORDS.

However out of the way they may be, the penitent is compelled to declare, on the spot and with some sort of connexion, the use he would make of three words, that may be named to him.

Example.

A lady asks of a gentleman,—

" Can you employ in my service, three things that I am about to name to you? "

" Madame, I can."

" We shall see. What would you do with a *locomotive,* a *flower-pot,* and a *tooth pick ?* "

* We cannot approve of this.   † This is impossible.

".I would leap astride the *locomotive* (holding on by the funnel), and heedless of the stoker's admonition, would put it to its utmost speed to carry me to your side. I would wrap the *flowerpot* carefully round with whity-brown paper,—for it should contain the Daffy-down-dilly, to be presented to you as an emblem of my love. And—inadequate as would be the weapon,—should no larger be at hand, I would make the *toothpick* reach my heart in case of your refusing to hear me."

THE FIRST LETTERS.

A certain number of letters are given to you, on which you are expected to found a speech (complimentary or the reverse, as may be desired) to the person furnishing them,—using each letter, in succession, as the commencement of a word.

The following are specimens ; the same collection of letters being employed with opposite intentions :—

W, y, n, t, y, m, g, i,

" *With your new triumphs, you may grow impatient.*"

" *Wish you not that you may get it?*"

T, s, s, n, y, s,

" *The sun shines.** No, 'tis your smile !*"

" *There's some satisfaction now that you're silent.*"

---

* Contractions of this description may be tolerated as one word.

THE TORN LETTER.

A lady presents to a gentleman a paper containing certain injurious phrases which he is accused of having written about her, and asks him if he can justify his infamous conduct. In order to do so, he proves that the letter has been torn in half, by adding to the end of each line certain other expressions, which he declares were to be found in the original manuscript, and which quite alter the meaning of the letter to one highly favorable to the lady.

Example.

"I confess to a great contempt for
Miss ———, whom I consider
the most ridiculous person
in the world. She is entirely
without sense, heart, or beauty,
The man whom she may
love is much to be pitied: the
man who could love her
if any such exist, is
entitled to our execration."

To make this somewhat scurrilous production palatable, the penitent has only to add to each line (in their place) the following words :—

—the idiots who cannot admire
—charming. Otherwise I should be

—breathing. She is without equal
—faultless. Only those who, being
—feel envious, could detract from her.
—prefer, and who cannot appreciate her
—crime of separating her from the
—sincerely, few would be responsible for ;
—not so much selfish thoughtlessness
— ? —

By placing which in proper connection with the lines given, the letter will be found to read as follows :—

"I confess to a great contempt for *the idiots who cannot admire* Miss ———, whom I consider *charming. Otherwise I should be* the most ridiculous person *breathing. She is without equal* in the world. She is entirely *faultless. Only those who, being* without sense, heart, or beauty, *feel envious, could detract from her.* The man whom she may *prefer, and who cannot appreciate her love,* is much to be pitied : the *crime of separating her from the* man who could love *her sincerely, few would be responsible for ;* if any such exist, is *not so much selfish thoughtlessness* entitled to our execration ?

BOUTS RIMES.

This being a French *Penitence,* by no means naturalized in this country, we have preserved the original title, for which we have no very good equivalent.

The facility of *rhyming* in the French language (so much greater than in our own) has given rise to several agreeable games depending upon the exercise of this faculty. Few of these would bear transplanting to English soil. The following, however, as a means of redeeming forfeits, is as well suited to this side of the Atlantic as the other.

A certain number of words, rhyming with each other, in pairs, are given to the penitent, who is expected to extemporize a corresponding number of verses, making use of the rhymes given for their termination. Care should, of course, be taken, to select words of the most disconnected meaning, so as to make the task as difficult as possible.

Examples.

The words given by a lady are,

THIEF,	HABIT,
GRIEF,	RABBIT,

The gentleman extemporizes :—*

> "Lady, I fear not to attack a *thief*,
> Bolder than brass, but now I own with *grief*,
> (You having stol'n my heart) my val'rous *habit*
> Fails, and I feel as timid as a *rabbit*.

HOT,	WHAT,
TALKER,	WALKER.

> "My task makes me feel rather *hot*,
> Being but an indifferent *talker*,

* A few minutes may be allowed for preparation. The *improvisatore* is not, however, allowed to keep supper waiting many hours in getting up his *impromptu*.

So for words, meanings, rhymes, in short *what*,
You demand, I refer you to *Walker*."*

These are, of course, silly enough, as such things must always appear, if considered apart from their legitimate object, that of contributing to the good humour of a society.

THE COMPLIMENT.

This is addressed, according to the orders received, to one or more, or even all persons in the room. If demanded in prose, it should be composed impromptu; if in verse, an extract from any song, applying to the person to be complimented, or the general tone of the society, will be sufficient.

THE EXCLUDED VOWEL.

The penitent is ordered to pay a compliment without making use of the letter A. The following is a specimen;—

"Either shut Miss Tomkins's eyes or put out the lights—*both* being superfluous."

Without E;—

---

* We beg to state distinctly, that the individual here intended is the author of the popular educational works on the English language,—not the shadowy person whose name is sometimes used to express incredulity or derision.

"Madam, yours is a divinity which no man could fail to worship."

Without I ;

"Talk of Clara, and not allude to *eyes !* Rather hard that! No matter—her eulogy may yet be pronounced with *ease* (E's)."

Without O ;

"What I intend saying is alike new and striking. Miss ——'s beauty is unequalled save by her wit."

Without U ;

> "Lady by all the stars I vow,
> To love thee dearest—then as now."

CHARADES.

You are expected to compose, upon a word given you secretly, a charade in prose, or (as is preferable) in verse.

Examples.

My first is useless without my second, which is of little value unless comprising the qualities of my whole.—HOUSE-WIFE.

> My *first* is very often reckon'd
> A name adapted to my *second,*
> But for the meaning of each *word,*
> I leave you to consult my *third.*
>
> JOHN-SON.

In the Eastern land where the nights are calm,
Where the rain is dew, and the air is balm—
When the silver moon is high,

Roused by the note the Bulbul sings
To the sleeping rose—*my first* upsprings
From her leafy couch, and on gossamer wings
    Sails through the clear blue sky.

When the autumn blasts through the valleys sweep,
And the brown leaves lie on the path knee deep,
    And the echoing woods, all day,
Ring with the crack of the gunshot fell—
Of pheasant or partridge plump the knell,
Woe to the wretch who in glade or dell
    May come in *my second's* way

A thoughtful boy, with a wild sea-shell,
Busies himself, as a mystic spell
    Its mysteries to unroll—
With a weapon sharp to extract what lies
Hidden within it—he gains the prize!
Model of patience to all the wise
    Who wish to get at *my whole!*

PERI-WINKLE.

The last is, of course, of two complicated a nature to be expected on an *impromptu* occasion.

The amusement may be prolonged by making all who " give up," or guess incorrectly the charades, pay fresh forfeits.

FORFEITS.*

THE interest of a game of forfeits is often marred at its conclusion, by the want of variety in the tasks set for the redemption of the various pledges. Those should not be of a commonplace or unmeaning description. There is very little amusement to be got from ordering a gentleman to kiss such or such a lady—to sing a song—to stand on one leg, &c. &c.

In " crying forfeits," not only should some degrees of intelligence or whimsicality be displayed in inventing the different acts of penitence ; they should also be adapted to the capacity of the indiviuals selected to execute them.

We will endeavour to indicate a considerable number

---

* As a great number of the following acts of Penitence depend upon the introduction of " kissing," to which, properly, an objection will exist in many societies, the writer begs to call attention to the note attached to the game of *The Wolf and the Lambs* (page 14,) and to repeat seriously what was then said in jest,—viz., that such amusements are only intended for societies where relationship or extreme intimacy will warrant such familiarity. It has not been considered expedient to separate them from the rest—a confidence in the good taste and sense of propriety of our readers rendering such a proceeding unnecessary.

that will be found no less amusing in the carrying out, than the games which have given rise to them.

BLOWING OUT THE CANDLE.

A candle is passed rapidly backwards and forwards before the mouth of the penitent, who has to blow it out during its passage. This is a more difficult feat than may be imagined.

THE CHAM OF TARTARY.

The penitent takes a candle—placing another in the hands of a person of different sex. Both advance to the extremity of the room. Then, they assume a lugubrious aspect and advance with measured steps towards each other. When they meet they raise their eyes to the ceiling, say a few words in the most sepulchral tone, and change places with each other—the most miserable and dejected expression of countenance being indispensable.

This ceremony is repeated as many times as there are phrases in their dialogue—which is as follows :—

The Gentleman.—Know you the dreadful news ?

The Lady.—Alas !

Gent.—The Cham of Tartary is dead.

Lady.—Alas ! Alas !

Gent.—Buried.

Lady.—Alas ! Alas ! Alas !

Gent.—Alas! Alas! A thousand times alas!

He cut his head off with a sword of brass!

Both finish their promenade quite overcome by their feelings, and resume their seats as gaily as they please.

THE PARROT.

The giver of a forfeit is supposed to be transformed to a parrot. The conditions of his situation are as follow :—

He must go round to all the players, and ask one after the other,—

" If I were your parrot, what would you teach me to say ?"

Each player answers as his fancy may dictate. If a lady say, " Kiss poor Polly," the supposed parrot puts the suggestion in practice, and his ordeal is at an end. If not, he must repeat exactly every answer before passing on to another person.

DUMMEY.

This consists in executing the acts of penitence ordained you by each member of the company, without speaking a word.

THE STATUE.

The penitent is placed, by each person in succession, in an uncomfortable or ridiculous posture—which he is not

E.BALDWIN ENG.

W. MOMBERGER.

KISSING THE CANDLESTICK.

allowed to quit, except to assume another, till he has completed the round.

A condition is sometimes added to this act—rather troublesome for the *statuary*. It is to use, for the purpose of placing the *statue* in the desired position, the hand opposite to that employed by his predecessor for the same purpose. Anybody neglecting this formality becomes statue himself.

KISSING THE CANDLESTICK.

When ordered to kiss the candlestick, you politely request a lady to hold the candle for you. As soon as she has it in her hand, she is supposed to be the candlestick ; and you, of course, kiss *her*.

THE DISAPPOINTMENT.

A lady advances towards the penitent as if to kiss him ; and when close to him, turns quietly round and allows the expected kiss to be taken by her nearest neighbour.

THE SPIRIT OF CONTRADICTION.

Do the direct contrary to what the different members of the company order you to.

THE BEGGAR.

A penitence to be inflicted on gentlemen only. The

penitent takes a staff, and approaches a lady. He falls on his knees before her, and, thumping his staff on the ground, implores " Charity." The lady, touched by the poor man's distress, asks him—"Do you want bread?" " Do you want water?" "Do you want a half-cent?" &c. &c. ; to all questions such as these the beggar replies by thumping his staff on the ground, impatiently. At length the lady says, " Do you want a kiss?" At these words, the beggar jumps up, and kisses the lady.

THE PILGRIM.

The Pilgrim is very like the Beggar. A gentleman conducts a lady round the circle, saying to each member of it, if a gentleman, " A kiss for my sister, and a morsel of bread for me!" If a lady, " A morsel of bread for my sister, and a kiss for me!" The bread is of no particular importance, but the kiss is indispensable.

SULKS.

A lady is ordered to sulk. She whispers in the ear of the Forfeit Crier the name of the person she chooses to kiss. All the gentlemen of the company then present themselves before her. She turns her back upon them all, in a pouting manner, until the arrival of the fortunate individual, whom she kisses.

We should remark, that gentlemen may sulk as well as ladies.

LANGUISHING.

The penitent is ordered into a corner to languish. This is done by simply saying, "I languish." She is then asked, "For whom do you languish?" and answers by naming any player of the opposite sex he may please, who is obliged to come and kiss him. The lady then languishes for a gentleman, who approaches her, and languishes for another lady, and so on, till all the players have been called from their places and form a line of a lady and a gentleman placed alternately. When the line is complete, the original languisher turns round, and goes to his seat, stopping on the way to kiss all the ladies in the row. The lady left at the top does the same to all the gentlemen—and so on, down to the last player, who, having no one to kiss, had better return to his seat as quietly as he came from it.

SO MANY YARDS OF KISSES.

The penitent is ordered to give so many yards of kisses to a lady or gentleman (as the case may be). This is done by taking the lady (or gentleman) to the centre of the room. Both then take hold of each other's hands, and extend them to their full length, as if "measuring ribbon," exchanging a kiss each time, to the number appointed.

THE CLOCK.

A player is condemned to transformation to a clock. He stands before the mantelpiece, and calls a player (of the opposite sex) to him. The person thus called upon, asks the "clock" what time it is. The clock replies, whatever hour he likes;—claiming the same number of kisses as he names hours of the day.

If approved of, the player who has asked the time takes the place of the clock, and calls upon another ; the original ceremony being repeated in turns by all the players of the company.

THE ARBOUR OF LOVE.

The lady (or gentleman) commanded to perform this act, conducts a person of the opposite sex to the centre of the room, where they join both hands, raising their arms in the form of an arbour. The lady then calls upon a gentleman, and the gentleman upon a lady, who must pass together under the arbour. But when they are just under it, the arms are lowered to bar their passage, and they are kept prisoners till they have kissed each other. This done, the arms are raised, and the imprisoned couple continue their *route*, then stop, and forming a *second* arbour, call upon another couple. This third couple pass under both arbours—paying the tribute already mentioned at each—and form a third arbour, calling upon another couple, and so on, till all the members of the company have been summoned. The last arbour being formed, the feat terminates, and all retire to their seats.

KISSING UNDER THE CANDLESTICK.

This consists in kissing a person over whose head you hold a candlestick.

TO KISS YOUR OWN SHADOW.

Place yourself between the light and the person you intend kissing, on whose face your own shadow will be thrown.

TO KISS THE ONE YOU LOVE BEST WITHOUT ITS BEING NOTICED.

Kissing all the ladies in the company one after another without any distinction.

THE CHANCE KISS.

The penitent takes from a pack of cards the four kings and the four queens, shuffles them, and, without looking at them, distributes them to a proportionate number of ladies and gentlemen. The gentleman finding himself possessed of the king of hearts kisses the lady holding the queen, and so on with the rest.

This is unsatisfactory and tantalizing enough for the poor penitent. He can, however, derive some little satisfaction from spoiling the fun of the others, by giving the kings to the most self-satisfied young gentlemen of the company, and the queens to any of their venerable female relations who may be present.

THE KNIGHT OF THE RUEFUL COUNTENANCE.

There are two ways of executing this penance. One consists simply in the penitent holding a lady on his knees for another gentleman to kiss.

The other is as follows :—

The knight is provided with a squire—in the person of a gentleman in the company, whom he leads round the assembled circle—the knight holding a candle and the squire a handkerchief.

The squire kisses all the ladies in turn, and after each kiss politely wipes the lips of the knight—a helpless and inactive spectator of his servant's satisfaction.

ARIADNE'S LEOPARD; OR, THE HOBBY HORSE.

The penitent, on his hands and knees, is obliged to carry round the room a lady who is seated on his back, and whom all the gentlemen (himself excepted) are privileged to kiss in turns.

THE SOFA.

The penitent places himself in the same position as for "Ariadne's Leopard," that is to say, on all fours. He, however, remains stationary, receiving on his back a lady and a gentleman, who sit comfortably down and exchange a kiss.

THE EXILE.

The penitent sent into exile takes up his position in the part of the room the most distant from the rest of the company—with whom he is forbidden to communicate. From there, he is compelled to fix the penance to be performed by the owner of the next forfeit, till the accomplishment of which he may on no account leave his place. This may be prolonged for several turns. The last penitent, as soon as he has acquitted himself satisfactorily, taking the place of the exile, and passing sentence on the next.

TO BE AT THE MERCY OF THE COMPANY.

This consists in executing whatever task each member of the company may like to impose upon you.

JOURNEY TO ROME.

The person whose forfeit is called, must go round to every individual in the company to tell them that he is

going on a journey to Rome, and to assure them if they
have any message or article to send to his Holiness the
Pope, he will feel great pleasure in taking it. Every
one must give something to the traveller, no matter how
cumbrous it may be or awkward to carry, (indeed the
more inconvenient the articles are the more it increases
the merriment,) until he is literally overloaded with presents. When he has gathered from all, he walks to a
corner of the room, puts the articles down, and so his
penance ends.

THE CUSHION.

The owner of the forfeit takes a cushion, and gives it
to one of the company, who then kneels down on the
floor, holds the cushion a little before him, and requests
the bringer to kneel down on it; as the latter attempts
to kneel, the former slides the cushion away, so that the
unlucky wight kneels on the carpet instead; should he,
however, be fortunate enough to kneel on the cushion at
once, he takes it to the next player; but if not, he must
continue his attempts until he is successful. The cushion
is to be given to every one in the room in rotation, and
the kneeling penance above described repeated before
each.

THE STATUE OF LOVE.

The player who owns the forfeit cried, takes a candle

in his hand, and is led by another to one end of the room, where he must stand and represent the Statue of Love ; one of the players now walks up, and requests him to fetch some lady, whose name he whispers in Love's ear ; the statue, still holding the candle, proceeds to execute his commission, and brings the lady with him ; she in turn desires him to fetch some gentleman, and so it continues till all have been summoned. The players brought up by Love, must not return to their seats, but stand in a group round Love's standing-place, until he has brought the last person in the company; when they hiss him most vigorously; and the forfeit terminates.

THE COUNTRY TABLE.

In this penance, the owner of the forfeit selects some one to be secretary, then kneels down upon his hands and knees on the floor, to represent the table, and his secretary takes his stand beside him. One of the company next dictates to the secretary, who should move his hand on the back of the kneeling player, as if he were writing a letter ; the dictator must call out " comma !" when he wishes that stop to be made, which the secretary responds to by making a motion with his finger on the " country table," resembling that stop ; a " semicolon," by giving a knock with his fist on the table and making a comma ; a " colon," by giving two knocks ; and a " full stop," by

one. For the sake of losing as little time as possible in
one forfeit, it is not necessary to request more than the
points or stops to be made on the "country table."

IN-DOOR SPORTS.

THREAD THE NEEDLE.

A number of boys all join hands, and the game is be-
gun by the outside players at each end of the line holding the following dialogue :—"How many miles to Baby-
lon?" "Three score and ten." "Can I get there by
candlelight?" "Yes, and back again." "Then open
the gates without more ado, and let the king and his men
pass through." The player and the one next to him at
the end of the line opposite the last speaker then raise
their joined hands as high as they can, to allow the
speaker to run under, and the whole line follow him, still
holding hands. This should be done, if possible, without breaking the line by letting the hands go, and is
styled "threading the needle." When all the boys have
passed through, the dialogue is repeated, except that the
player who before replied, now asks the question, and
runs between the opposite players, the others following
as before.

THE GENTEEL LADY.

Those who make a mistake in this difficult game must have a paper horn twisted fantastically, and so placed in their hair that it will shake about at the least motion. Two mistakes receives two horns, three mistakes three horns, &c. When a large number of twisted papers are prepared, one begins the game by saying to the one who stands at her right hand, "Good morning, genteel lady, always genteel ; I, a genteel lady, always genteel, come from that genteel lady, always genteel (here she points to the left), to tell you that she owns an eagle with a golden beak." The next one attempts to repeat the phrase, word for word, only adding, "an eagle with golden beak *and silver claws.*" If she make the slightest mistake in repeating the sentence, she must have a paper horn put in her hair ; and her next neighbour takes up the phrase thus, to the one on her right hand : "Good morning, genteel lady, always genteel ; I, a genteel lady, always genteel, come from that *horned* lady, always horned (pointing to the one on her left), to say that she has an eagle with golden beak, silver claws, and *a lace skin.*" Perhaps this one will make three mistakes before she gets through the sentence, if so, the next says, "Good morning, genteel lady, always genteel ; I, a genteel lady, always genteel, come from that three horned lady, always three horned, to say that she has an eagle with a golden beak, silver claws, lace skin, and *diamond eyes.*" If she should happen to receive four horns for as many mistakes, her next neighbour would say, after repeating the first part of the sentence, " I come from the four horned lady, always four horned, to say that she has an eagle with a golden beak, silver claws, lace skin, diamond eyes, and *purple feathers.*"

Thus it goes round the circle ; but the second time it goes round, it is still more difficult and more droll. By that time, the chance is everybody will have a greater or less number of horns ; and those who repeat, must remember exactly, or else they obtain another horn. Thus, if your left hand neighbour has two horns, you have three horns, and your right hand neighbour has four, you must say, " Good morning, four horned lady, always four horned ; I, a three horned lady, always three horned, come from that two horned lady, always two horned (pointing to the left), to say that she has an eagle," &c.

By the time the game is finished, the children's heads are generally ridiculous enough. To make it more funny, the speaker sometimes pretends to cry when she calls *herself* three horned, and laughs when she calls her *neighbour* four horned. This is a French game, played both by boys and girls.

THE BIRD-SELLER.

The company are seated in a circle, one only standing in the centre, and she is called the bird-seller. She stoops down to each one, and they whisper in her ear the name of whatever bird they choose to take for themselves. These she must carefully remember. If she fears she shall forget them, she must write them with a pencil. Then she must repeat them aloud, thus : " Gentlemen and ladies, I have in my collection an Eagle, a Swan, a Bird of Paradise, a Crow, a Wren, a Magpie," &c. &c. If the lists are written down, she must be careful not to read them in the same succession she wrote them ; if she does, the players will easily conjecture to whom the name belongs, and that would not be fair. After the list is read, the Bird-seller must ask each one, "To which of my birds will you make your bow ? To which will you tell a secret ? From which will you pluck a feather ?" Each one replies according to her taste ; perhaps she will answer, "I will bow to the eagle, tell my secret to the Bird of Paradise, and pluck a feather from the Jay." Those who happen to have a feather plucked from them, must pay a forfeit ; the one to whom a secret is to be imparted, has something whispered in her ear ; and a bow is made where a bow is promised ; little girls sometimes substitute a courtesy for a bow, when there are no boys in the

game. No one must make her bow, or tell a secret, or
pluck a feather, from the bird whose name she has chosen
for herself. A forfeit must be paid, if any one names a
bird that is not in the list. The forfeits are not paid, and
the bows are not made, &c. until the Bird-seller has asked
her questions all round the circle ; if she cannot then
remember what each one has chosen, they must put her
in mind of it. If one escapes without having a feather
plucked, she becomes the Bird-seller of the next game.
If nobody is lucky enough to escape, the one who sat at
the right hand of the Bird-seller, before she rose, is
chosen.

THE FRENCH ROLL.

In the beginning, some one is chosen to perform the
part of *purchaser*. She stands apart, while the others arrange themselves in a long file, one behind the other, each
taking hold of her neighbour's sleeve. The little girl
who happens to be at the head is a *baker ;* all the others
form the *oven*, with the exception of the last one, who is
called the French Roll. The *baker* does not keep her
station long, as you will see. As soon as the file is
formed, the *purchaser* comes up to the *baker*, and says,
" Give me my roll." The baker answers, " It is behind
the oven." The purchaser goes in search of it, and at
the same moment the little girl at the end, who is called

the roll, lets go her companion's sleeve, and runs up on the side opposite the purchaser, crying when she starts, "Who runs? who runs?" Her object is to get in front of the baker before the purchaser can catch her. If she succeeds, she becomes baker, and the little girl who stood next above her becomes the roll; if she does not succeed, she has to take the place of the purchaser, and the purchaser becomes baker. This play is a very active, and rather a noisy one. When the company get fully engaged in it, there is nothing heard but " Give me my roll!" "It is behind the oven." "Who runs? who runs?" As they do not run very far, they can run very quick, without fatigue; and as they are changing places all the time, each one has a share of the game. Sometimes they make it a rule, that every one who is caught in trying to get before the baker, shall pay a forfeit; but when they stop to pay forfeits, the game is not so animated.

CHAIRING THE LEG.

Having put your left foot on the lowest back rail of a strong chair, firmly placed so as not to be liable to slip, carefully try to pass your right leg over the back of the chair, and bring it to the floor between your left leg and the chair : in performing this trick, it is not allowable to touch the chair with your hands.

PROSTRATE AND PERPENDICULAR.

Cross your arms on your body, lie down on your back, and then get up again, without using either your elbows or hands in the feat.

THE STOOPING STRETCH.

Chalk a line on the floor, and place on it the outer edge of the right foot, at a little distance behind which, put the left heel on the line. Bend down and pass the right hand between your legs, under the right knee, and, with a piece of chalk in your right hand, draw a line on the floor, as far from the former line as you possibly can; yet not so far but that you can easily recover yourself without touching the ground with your hands, or removing your feet from the line. Provided you keep your feet properly placed, your body may project beyond the chalked line.

THE TANTALUS TRICK.

Let a person stand with his back and heels close to a wall, then place a shilling on the floor, at a little distance in front of him, and tell him he shall have the money if he can take it up without advancing his heels from the wall. Although at first sight it appears very easy to perform this trick, yet it is impracticable; as it is impossible to stoop in consequence of the proximity to the wall.

ANOTHER TANTALUS TRICK.

Place the left leg and foot, and left cheek, against a wall ; then lift the right leg slowly, endeavour to touch the left knee with it, and stand steadily in that position.

KNUCKLE DOWN.

Place the toes against a line chalked on the floor, kneel down and get up again without using the hands, your feet having the same position as at first.

DOT AND CARRY TWO.

This feat is to be performed by three players—whom we will name, A, B, C,—in the following manner :—Let A stand between B and C, and stooping down, pass his right hand behind the left thigh of B, and grasp B's right hand ; he should next pass his left hand behind the right thigh of C, and grasp *his* left hand ; B and C should then each pass an arm round the neck of A, who, rising by degrees, will be able to lift the others from the floor.

THE TRIUMPH.

This is a very excellent feat, and requires great practice to perform it adroitly : put your arms behind you and bring the palms of your hands together, the fingers downward, and the thumbs next your back ; then turn your hands, keeping the tops of the fingers close to your back, and the palms still together, until the ends of the fingers are brought between your shoulders, pointing toward your head, and the thumbs outside.

TO TAKE A CHAIR FROM UNDER YOU WITHOUT FALLING.

To perform this feat, lie along on three chairs, the middle chair being lighter than at each end. Throw up your chest, keep your shoulders down, and your limbs as stiff as you possibly can ; then take the centre chair from under your body, carry it over, and replace it under your body on the opposite side.

THUMB SPRING.

Place the inside of the thumb on the edge of a table, taking care that neither the fingers nor the palm of the hand touch it ; next move your feet as far back as you possibly can, and then taking a spring from the thumb, recover your standing position, without shifting your feet forward. It will facilitate the spring, if you rock yourself to and fro, three or four times, before you take it.

THE FLYING BOOK.

Hold between your ancles and the inner side of your feet a book ; then by kicking up backward with both your feet, jerk the book over your head.

LEAP BEFORE YOU LOOK.

, Take a strong chair, with so narrow a back, that you can bestride it without difficulty : stand on the seat, put your hands on the top rail of the back, and rest your knees against the middle rail ; then push the chair forward until it rest only on its hind legs, and before you lose your balance, jump from the seat, so that when you alight on the floor, you still hold the back rail in your hand. In all feats with chairs, it is necessary to use great caution in making the first attempts.

THE LONG REACH.

Chalk a line on the floor, and place the toes of both feet on it, being careful that they are not beyond it ; then, throw forward either the right or left hand, so far that you can easily spring back and regain your upright position without either moving the feet from the line, touching the floor with the hands in throwing them forward, or in springing back. Having thus stretched as far forward as you possibly can, whilst supporting the body upon one hand, with the other chalk a line on the floor. You may, in order to bring your body lower, move your feet backward from the line marked on the floor, and by so doing you will be enabled to make a much greater stretch than you could otherwise have done. If you can chalk two lines, your own length apart, it is a tolerably good stretch ; but with a little practice, you may chalk much further. Some persons, in performing this feat, rest upon their elbows instead of their hands.

THE CRADLE OF LOVE.

This little game has exercise and graceful movement to recommend it. All, except two, take their places as in a contra-dance; the two who are thus left out join hands, and attempt to dance between the couple at the foot ; the couple join hands and inclose them ; and the prisoners are not allowed to escape, till each has turned round and kissed the one behind her. In this way they dance through every couple in the set. When performed with ease and animation, it is very pleasing. Sometimes this is used as a forfeit.

THE END.

Lightning Source UK Ltd.
Milton Keynes UK
UKHW011409181218
334208UK00005B/242/P